# Striper Strategies

# Striper Strategies

## D. J. MULLER

Illustrations by Mark Jolliffe

Burford Books

Printed in the United States of America.

10   9   8   7   6   5   4   3   2   1

Library of Congress Cataloging-in-Publication Data is available at
the Library of Congress.

# Contents

# Dedication

To my life-long friend, Steve Daniels, my brother of the surf. We cut our teeth together chasing stripers from the sandy beaches of Jersey to the beautiful Vineyard. There was no short cut in the learning curve back then, no internet, so we read books, and we fished. After much pain we finally got it down. You have been a great friend to me. Thanks for everything.

John Haberek, I guess your work down here was done and the Good Lord thought that it was time for you to fish the Great Surf. You're gone, but your spirit still burns strong.

To the women of my life, Anna and Hillary. I cannot imagine my life without you!

To my pop, Herbert, and my brother, Rich, we spent many an evening fishing the docks.

To Christ, who daily bestows upon us goodness and strength.

# Acknowledgments

The writing of the book is easy compared to writing of the acknowledgements because you know that just as sure as the sun will rise in the eastern sky tomorrow that you will inevitably forget some one important. If and when I do that, call me and we can chat for a little while or maybe go fishing.

First I want to thank my wife Anna for another year of putting up with me and my face stuck to the computer screen and for putting up with me saying, "What? Did you say something?" every time she talked to me while I was typing or doing research. And of course for putting up with the "couple days" I went fishing last year.

I want to thank Hillary for her advice and patience—she helped out a lot on this book.

To my pal, a top notch bassman and a great illustrator to boot, Mark Jolliffe thanks for his unbelievable drawings and for his patience with my constant suggestions. I won't forget that night we slept on the beach and almost froze to death. You're a good friend!

To Bill Sistad, another great bassman and like a brother to me, we did a lot of work getting this book together. If we worked on the book more instead of fishing every night I would have got it done a lot faster.

To my neighbor and buddy Gammer the Hammer, his support is great, his intensity and drive . . . amazing. "Let's go hangout in the garage."

To Jim Murtagh, "Murty!!" Thanks for being a good bud. "You want to go to Connecticut?"

Pete Barrett it is a pleasure working with you and your professionalism not to mention your great disposition.

The Jersey Shore Surfcaster—what a special group of surfcasters and friends. Carhart the mayor and Peterson my right-hand man.

To Lou Rivetti, thanks for the insights, I hope the surf-gods bestow on you a lunker crab fish.

To Ron Bala—you are a good friend and keep one of the best surf shops on the East Coast, Brian's Fisherman's Supply. "Clams, clams, clams!"

To Paul Comerford and the warm and happy crew that hangs out at Grumpy's Bait and Tackle, we had way too many laughs! The place is a home away from home. Thanks for all of it.

While I am in "shop" mode I would like to thanks Pat Abate at River's End Tackle for all his help and insights, what a wealth of history and knowledge . . . and thanks for the "skins."

Rich Karpowicz, thanks for everything you do, stop making me laugh.

To all of my fishing posse, the guys I go to battle with: Andy Schmidt, Geoff Turner, Pat Leonard, Johnny Green, Gregg Oliver, Bob McGinley, "Football Jack," Jack LaGrossa, Shel. What a great group of relentless basshounds.

To Bobby Matthews thanks for your continued support, you are always happy to help out.

To Don Guimelli and Steve Adams thanks for your friendship and support.

Steve and Don Musso thanks you for your willingness and time.

Captain Alex Majewski thanks for the live-well tips.

Dave Anderson I always appreciate our conversations.

George Tompkins, you are one of the best all around bassmen that I know.

Crazy Al—you are a special friend. I'll get you for putting that pepper in my spaghetti sauce!

I also want to recognize Big Rock, Dilly Dock, Big Joe, Bill Lellis, Swiss, TNT, Gary Hull, Hutch and Gary Soldati, you guys are great!

# Introduction

Casting a small offering into the vast, endless ocean is in and of itself a simple task, however, if it is a large striped bass that you want to catch, everything from that point forward becomes quite a bit more complicated. The striper, the great king of the skinny water, finds its greatest comfort so close to the dry shore that a surf man standing on terra firma has a legitimate shot at catching one. If you make your moves with calculation and if you study the movements and habits of the great bass, then add to the mix a perfectly presented offering at a carefully chosen time, you will catch some good fish. This is the essence of our chase, of our passion.

As time marches ever forward, the minutes run to hours, the hours to days, the days to weeks, the weeks to years, and the world around us seems to move at the speed of sound and our technology at the speed of light. Yet as much as everything has developed in the past decades, our father's and forefather's need for recreation, to play, is still strong and for fishermen, that means we must fish. Remember the old saying, "Stop the world I want to get off?" Well, for many us surfcasting is a rest area on the Thruway of Life. Standing before a raging sea equipped with only the bare necessities gets us so pumped up for what lies ahead that our immediate troubles and concerns of the moment flee, and our gaze falls upon what swims before us in the water. It is a time and a place where we go to escape the hectic daily grind of life, it is a place where we find solace. Man has gone fishing for hundreds of years at the ocean's edge in search of a challenge against a formidable adversary, and for much needed tranquility. I do understand why.

Learning is fun, especially when it is accompanied by success. This book is about methods, options and specific techniques for catching striped bass. When you have options you can then formulate competent and legitimate strategies. If you go fishing without a strategy you can't expect much. Information on the various ways to catch bass will aid you in your challenge and bring you the happiness of the take—the actual catching of the fish.

Above all things it is terribly important that you remember to enjoy your trip down the surfcasting highway. I see way too many people stressed out over what is supposed to be our "leisure." Don't forget to stop and smell the proverbial flowers along the path and don't forget to enjoy the fish that you do battle with. I don't consider surfcasting my social outlet by any means, but there are times when you go with friends, and when you do, make sure you "lock in" the good times.

For example I occasionally catch up to Crazy Al and we do a couple of tides from time to time. I must say there is no one else I've met who rivals his intensity, concentration-level and skill. I like that kind of seriousness, yet when we are not actually fishing we sure have a good time full of laughs, ball-busting and in-depth conversation. We are there strictly to fish and a good fish sure makes for good memories, but the times when you laugh so hard your stomach cramps up are also memorable. Be sure to enjoy the good times too. After all it's only fishing.

It is my hope the contents in this book will bring you a fraction of the satisfaction that striper fishing from the surf has brought to me. I write to give back to the sport I love. Enjoy.

# Striper Strategies

# 1
# THE ART OF PERSUASION

I can remember quite clearly my father, my brother and me negotiating the cumbersome rocks on Manasquan Inlet's north jetty one late afternoon. We were fishing the ocean side about 100 yards from the pocket just beyond the third wave. I was always so psyched up to go fishing with my brother and father. When my father brought home two new rods and reels earlier that afternoon, my eyes lit up like a "normal" kid would react when his parents pulled a new car into the driveway. We baited up with fresh spearing purchased at Fisherman's Cove, the tackle shop just inside the inlet run by Clem Danish and his sons. They always had crisp fresh-caught spearing, never frozen.

My father would cast out and we would hold our rods waiting for a good strike. This particular day my father hooked a fish, and he was a bit excited because of the fight it was putting up. It wasn't the typical sea robin or sundial. He finally pulled up a nice fluke that went about 3 pounds. My eyes must have been as big as hubcaps; I could not believe what we had just pulled from the ocean waters. It was my first exposure to the "art of persuasion" in regards to a catching gamefish.

A few years later I walked out into a black Bay Head morning and made my way out onto the groin at Osborne Avenue. I was as green as a greenhorn could be. I had heard that Smokey Joe Red Fins had been taking some bass so I clipped one on and went to work. I was so ready to catch my first striper I could hardly contain my eagerness. Sure enough the hit came about 20 minutes later and I fought the titan with all my might! A short while later I beached a 1-pound bluefish. It wasn't a bass but it was a triumphant day and a glorious week to follow as I reveled in my accomplishment. I had fooled my first fish on an artificial and I was so stoked!

Yes, I am laughing now, but looking back at the road on which I was about to travel, the road every surfcaster ventures down on his way to self-sufficiency, it was an integral part of my bass-hunter development. My confidence level sky-rocketed that day. As a surfcaster confidence in your ability to fool a fish is more than half the battle.

Years later I watched my spiked rod go down hard and bend as though it would break. I abruptly ended my conversation with the guy

*The sunrise in the east brings new opportunities for the surfcaster.*

next to me, grabbed hold of the rod and wrestled it from its holder. The spool was already draining line at full bore as I pulled it out of the spike. Only a few days earlier I had caught a 42-pound bass and the day after that my wife had a 40. This fish seemed bigger. As a precaution I came back hard to be sure that the hook was set deep into the jowls of the fish. I knew immediately that this fish was of considerable substance.

It shot out 120 yards without hesitation. My forehead began to sweat small beads of panic as the thrill of "Fish on!" was beginning to look like "fish gone." My line capacity was getting dangerously low. The great fish finally stopped and my hopes began to grow—until the fish decided to take off again. I had to walk down the beach quickly as the great fish made a beeline dead north and off to my left. She was out at 45 degrees and bolting parallel to the beach, and I could not afford to stop so I walked as fast as I could to keep up with her. She stopped once again and I began to horse a reluctant fish towards me. The pressure grew with every turn of the reel. I scolded myself, "Don't let this one get away Muller. You'll never forgive yourself!" At the same time I felt good and in control. I knew I had a fish of considerable substance on the business end. It was a trophy but I did not yet know how big. I concentrated, remained confident and in control, and I knew exactly what I needed to do with this fish.

A small crowd had assembled and followed me down the beach, a fishing buddy nicknamed Jazz ran beside me yelling words that I wasn't hearing. I was 100 percent focused on my task. The fish came unwillingly but I worked her patiently until finally I saw a good-sized dorsal fin break water as she breached the surface running parallel to the beach. Luckily for me this was a "dusk" fish lit up by the sun and I was able to observe the entire battle, not just feel it.

When I got a good look at her my mouth went to cotton but my determination grew. Time suddenly stood still in what seemed like a two-hour movie at the Loews Cinema where each of my bad surf-experiences haunted me from the past. I saw all of the big fish that I had lost to angler incompetence, equipment failure or just bad luck. All I needed was some popcorn with light butter and a soda. I saw the big bass that rolled at the jetty's edge one night scaring the crap out of me, and then with a mighty headshake threw the plug into the air. I saw the big bass that took a clam late one May morning and ran out 100 yards to a boat full of unsuspecting fishermen. She broke water and swept her tail on the surface

*The battle with a great fish is what every surfcaster longs for. Andy Schmidt battles a 30-pound bass.*

throwing a huge spray onto the back of the boat, the guys all yelled and pointed at the fish before she deep-sixed and came off leaving me only to consider what might have been. Then there was the rigged-eel bass that rolled and broke me off at the Shark River Inlet's north jetty pocket. I saw them all!

I remembered a bass that at Mackerel Cove in Jamestown ate an eel on a hot July night. It swam between my legs, broke my rod and then was gone. Oh, and the huge Vineyard bass that October night at Squibnocket on the black Danny plug that was still wet from the paint I had sprayed only hours before I went out. The ghosts of my past had all paid me a visit and I felt like Ebenezer Scrooge on Christmas Eve.

My arms were tired but pure adrenaline was compensating for my fatigue. I watched and prepared for my critical wash up. I yelled at Jazz, "Whatever happens don't touch that fish! Stand back! Get away!! I don't need your help," I let him know in no uncertain terms, yet he was poised to pounce. The wave crested and I came back hard trying to get the great fish up into position, the wave rose and crashed, and the fish, at the last second, found some extra fight and dove back down into the bottom of the wave. I did not get it where it had to be, the wave crashed and the fish washed only halfway up before the water started to recede.

Not listening, Jazz ran down to grab the monster despite my cry for abandonment. I watched as the fish washed back into the surf. I remember seeing Jazz jump to miss the fish but when doing so he hit the great fish in the head with his knee, pushing both my temperature and blood pressure skyward. The next wave crashed on the fish and it disappeared back into the wash as did Jazz who, while trying to jump over the fish, fell backwards into the ocean. I still remember watching him get swallowed up and disappear into the water, doing the Nes-Tea plunge. I could not help but laugh at his foolishness.

I lifted my rod tip and again felt the heaviness of the great fish. It was still there despite Jazz's momentary lack of reason. I again lifted the fish into the back of the wave and the crest lifted her as I pulled back hard. She was up top of the cresting wave and as the wave collapsed I applied more pressure. The fish was perfectly delivered onto the relatively steep slope of sand. I quickly went down and slipped my hand into her gill and slid her up to safety. It was at this point when Jazz and I uttered profan-

*A fooled bass soon to be released to swim and fight another day. Mark Jolliffe sports a mid 20-pound fish that fell for a snag-and-dropped bunker.*

ities incoherently while staring down acknowledging the size of this big girl. It was of incredible size and girth. I had to take a minute to apologize to the women and children that were present. I honestly did not realize what I was saying.

I immediately dragged the fish back up the beach 75 yards to where I started and where I had left all my equipment. The Berkeley Digital scale read 51.5! I knew I had to get this fish weighed on a good scale right now. By tomorrow it might be 49.99999 and that doesn't count as a 50 pounder. I hauled the fish up and over the dunes leaving all my equipment on the beach. I put the bass in the cooler in back of my truck. I knew the nearest shop would be closing in 15 minutes so I had no time to waste!

I made it to the shop and the fish hit the scale at 51 pounds even. The rest can be left for hearsay or legend or water cooler talk, whatever! It was a memorable day and a gleaming example of how a specific method of persuasion worked for me. The right place at the right time using the right technique. On this day it worked to the utmost.

## STRIPER AMBUSH

A large striper sits in ambush behind a rock pile at a warm fast-moving outflow. She is waiting for a school of herring or squid, or perhaps a big eel, to come dumping out of the river, the conveyor belt that brings dinner. She hears a distant sound in the calm water behind her, which instantly draws her interest. It sounded like the splash of a large baitfish breaking the surface of the water, perhaps wounded and struggling. In an instant her lateral line detects the vibration of this fish in distress. She turns her nose out of the current and heads into calmer water beside the rockpile. She is hungry.

Her large body moves in the direction of the vibration and she senses an easy meal nearby. As she moves closer the vibration gets stronger and as she homes in, she also hears a series of clacking-ticking sounds so she moves more quickly toward the potential meal. Her sense of aggression heightens, her dorsal fin now fully erect as she prepares to attack whatever is "calling" her. It's very close by, but she still cannot see it in the murky saltwater. Suddenly she sees the silhouette and makes an immediate decision, rolls up over the bait, quickly turns her large body and then swallows it whole. An easy meal is always rewarding.

Not far away a seasoned jetty jock feels the hard hit of a bass yet he keeps reeling, he knows better than to stop until the line comes tight. He feels the strike and comes back hard with his rod, and the surface explodes with a crashing sound that cuts through the stillness of the night. Hooks of the bottle plug dig deep into the jaw of the large striper as the angler leans back against the bent rod. The big fish heads for deep water and safety and herein lies a classic battle between two master hunters.

## THE WELL-BALANCED SURFCASTER, IS THE BEST SURFCASTER

If you want to be a truly great surfcaster, not a one-dimensional surfcaster, you have to be well versed and well prepared to fish each of the various techniques for catching stripers. You must be forever versatile. You must be able to move from being a great plug fisherman, to an accomplished chunker, to a wily eeler. If for some reason you commit to only one way of catching stripers then there is no way that you can be a completely efficient hunter or a quality bass man.

*The thrill of a good fish, a picture is worth a thousand words. Bill Sistad better check his rear hook.*

To catch the great striped bass you have to know what they are feeding on, when they want it and how to offer it to them so they are tempted to eat it. The striped bass is forever adapting to its surroundings, its environment and its constantly-changing food supplies; you also need to constantly adapt as a surfcaster.

In the chapters that follow, I will provide the ground work so you, the striped bass fisherman, can learn and execute the techniques that will one day make your dreams come true. You will only become good, however, not just by reading these words or beating on your computer's keyboard at the striper websites, but by applying these words as you fish. Roll up your sleeves, get on the beach and make the casts. You learn by doing. Knowledge without experience is just knowledge. Knowledge not applied is wasted, unless used. Knowledge mixed with a good dose of experience is what will make you good!

Catching a striper is the ultimate high for me. It makes me feel good inside. I guess the years and the experiences have done little to quench my desire to catch bass because the more I catch the stronger is my desire to catch more bass, so I push myself harder. When I don't catch I also drive myself harder based on my shortcomings. Analyzing the situation, figuring out the best strategy is the art of fooling fish. It's an enjoyable game that I love to play and it keeps me coming back for more.

To fool a small bass, for me, is simply play. I enjoy it immensely but it is the true cow that keeps me awake at night, that fills my thoughts during drives to work, that causes my mind to drift when I am in conversation about less important things. The cow bass are the hardest to fool, thus they bring the big rewards from the outside; compliments and fuss by on-lookers or surf brothers, perhaps a picture for the local newspaper. These are all nice but the greater satisfaction comes from within me, a payoff that no one understands but me or a fellow bass man. It's the satisfaction that I fooled a great fish that is the ultimate achievement for me as a surfcaster.

There is an added satisfaction, a bonus if you will, following a valiant battle with one of these kings of the surf, and that is the reward of watching one swim away, a prisoner set free. To watch it stroke its wide tail and accelerate into the dark mysterious night waters from which it came brings the pursuit and capture full circle. It's very gratifying to say the very least. There is a very short list of things that are better than this.

# 2

# SWIMMING THE ARTIFICIALS

catch striped bass on everything and anything; bunker chunks, eels, crabs, live bait and more, but anyone who has ever been in my garage probably thinks for sure that I am one of those artificial purist dudes. The rafters over my workbench are loaded with lures of plastic, rubber and wood. Just about every type of artificial fishing lure is hanging there, and in just about every color, shade and scale pattern variation, including the latest new colors and the favorites from years past.

Having just one of each can't be enough. What if I lose it? And, obviously, I need some back-ups, so I have about 29 of each! Okay, I'm being a bit facetious, but I do have a good collection of lures for every surf situation imaginable. I love catching fish on artificials!

I get a lot of questions about the lure collection hanging from my garage ceiling. The most often is, "Why so many?" The first few times I was asked this question, I laughed it off, slightly embarassed, thinking of myself as some kind of a plug freak or insecure glutton; but as I thought about it more and more, my answer has become, "Well, I bought them one or two at a time and I had very specific motives or scenarios for buying each one."

When I buy plugs it is for specific situations that I have in mind, and when I look at an individual plug hanging from the rafters, I say, "Ah yes, I remember when I bought that one," or I remember the night that it was a hot plug in Montauk and I didn't have the right color or size and I vowed to never let that happen again. Each plug has either a time or a place designated for it. I need them all!

When it comes to artificials you can never have enough, but let's face it, at the end of the day you probably have five that are your go-to lures, the lures that you would stake your reputation on, the lures you'd bet your paycheck on. It comes down to the simple premise of believing in what you have. When you believe, you feel good; when you feel good you fish better.

*The number of lures and colors available is amazing. The hit of a nice bass on a surface swimmer at first light is as good as it gets.*

I am sure that you have played the game in your head "If I could only take one plug, which would it be?" Don't be shy, we've all had this thought. When I think about it I say to myself, "Oh, man, how about that night we beat em up good on Bombers, but then there was that week of the needlefish bass, then again there was the bass in the boulder fields on metal-lips a couple years back." It's hard to pick just one plug as the best. This is why we have 12 slots in our plug bag; there is no one magic plug, and that is why we have so many different scenarios that call for different options. The plug selection also adds to the strategy and intrigue of striper fishing.

## THE MYSTIQUE OF ARTIFICIALS

What is it about artificial baits or lures that attracts fish? Did you ever wonder about that? A piece of wood or plastic with hooks hanging from it? What would you do if suddenly there was a knock at your door, you went to the door and saw a man-like robot standing there waiting to talk to you, perhaps looking a bit like the Tin Man from the Wizard of Oz? If he asked you to come outside, would you? Not in a million years!! You would know instantly that something was weird and your defenses would be sky high.

So what is it that makes a fish that lives in an underwater environment see a piece of rubber, plastic or wood with hooks and with strange colors on it decide that it is okay to eat that thing?

I think back to what Captain Al Ristori wrote in the Dedication of one of his books where he made reference to himself being absent from

*The love of the surf. Rich Karpowicz battles a fish on a cold and stormy Saturday morning in November.*

his family and home many times while he was out "trying to outwit crea-
tures with brains the size of a pea." Yes, I am afraid that bass are not terribly smart. They are instinctive beasts that we give way too much credit
to, but that's the challenge with artificials—getting a striped bass to eat our
offering is pleasurably entertaining.

This book has four chapters on fishing with artificial lures; surface
plugs, sub-surface swimmers, metals and soft-plastics. I feel it is important
that I emphasize several things that pertain to all the artificials you will
use in your life in the suds. The first thing I tell newcomers or fishermen
who I work with while guiding is that it is of the utmost importance
that you stay in constant contact or "touch" with your lure 100 percent
of the time once you catch up to it after the cast by reeling in the slack
line. It is the most important aspect of fishing with fakes.

Your lure must be an extension of you. You must be able to feel every
wiggle and wobble, you need to know when a fish hits ever so lightly or
when a fish brushes by your lure. When you lose contact with the plug,
how will you know when a fish hits, or when you are on the bottom, or
have seaweed wrapped around your hook? Your lure will tell you when
you are in the strong current of a rip or the slower current of an eddy just
off the rip. The lure you are using is your underwater "eye" that gathers
and transmits information to you. If you want to be good, "contact" is a
discipline that you must master.

The second point is that you as the angler *must* know and be intimate
with *every* plug you throw into the surf. To simply walk out to the water's
edge and blindly cast a lure you are unfamiliar with will not do much for
your presentation, your productivity or your confidence. You want to
know how every plug will work at fast or slow retrieve speeds, calm or
rough surf, in what situation does it work "best" and what are the small
tricks with that plug that entice strikes, such as a simple twitch or the
sweep of the rod, or just letting the lure sit still for a few seconds before
continuing the retrieve.

What does all this talk of contact and intimacy mean for the surfcaster? It breeds confidence and confidence is everything; not only for
fishing the "artificial" side of surfcasting, but for all the aspects of surfcasting. You must be confident in your strategy and your approach to
catching fish. You must *expect* to catch when you go. If you have a well-
made plan and you are well prepared, you should then catch fish.

*Staying in contact with your lure the entire time is a must when fishing with artificials. It is when you begin to feel every move the lure makes that your productivity will increase.*

Confidence in your approach is knowing for a fact that if a fish sees your offering it will take it or you will fool it. With certain lures, I just know that if a bass sees it, it will take the lure. That's confidence!

## HARDWARE CHECK

Another thing that is very important for you to do is to make sure that your hooks and split rings are up to snuff, especially on the big plugs that are used to catch truly big bass. I check the split rings on all of my plastic plugs, such as Bombers, poppers and Red-Fins. If they look thin, rusty or questionable they get replaced. I leave no room for failure. On my big bass plugs I put the splits to the ultimate garage test. The hook is clamped tight into the bench vice and I pull hard as I can. If the split ring bends or pops off, it gets replaced. I like Wolverine triple coil Super Rings or if those are too large to fit through the hook eye, loop or barrel swivel of the plug, I like Owner Hyper Wire split rings.

If the hooks don't look sound I give them the pliers test. If they twist or bend easily, they're gone. I like the VMC 4X and 6X as replacements. On some plugs it pays to increase the hook size to give the plug a different action, for example, a larger hook will make it swim a little deeper or slower with a little less side-to-side action.

## TACKLE AND EQUIPMENT CHOICES

The tackle and equipment you use to fish with artificial lures depends upon many variables including the lure size and weight, how you are fishing (swimming plug with a steady retrieve, pencil popper with an erratic retrieve), where you are fishing and the type of beach or sea conditions.

*When bass are feeding on peanuts in the fall surf, a medium-size rod and reel and medium-size lures work like a charm.*

To throw big lures, such as a 3-ounce popper or big metal-lip swimmer a long distance, you'll need a rod with muscle. An undersized rod will result in rod breakage, which is never any fun and only leads to frustration. When throwing big lures use a rod rated for up to 4 to 6 ounces, and generally a longer rod will also provide more leverage, such as a 10- to 11-foot rod. As an example, a Lamiglas GSB120 1L or M custom-built rod or the XS101MS factory rod are good choices, and the G. Loomis SUR 1324S 11-foot rod is another favorite. When casting long distances you will need a high-capacity reel such as a Van Staal 200, 250, 275 or 300, or a ZeeBass ZX27. A Penn 704 or 706Z will also carry enough line. I prefer 50-pound Sufix braid when casting big plugs.

For smaller surface swimmers, I like to go smaller and lighter with a 9-foot rod being ideal, or perhaps even going down to an 8-foot rod with the proper lure weight rating. If I am doing a lot of "short" work, like short casts from jetties, a 9-foot rod like the Lamiglas XS91MHS factory rod or GSB 108M blank to build a custom rod would be suitable. Both rods have a good feel to them with plenty of power for casting and enough backbone to lift fish to where I can grab it.

For quiet rivers and back waters, or for open unobstructed beach in good weather, I like to go down to a 7-foot light-action rod. I still use my 7-foot St. Croix Ben Doer Series surf rod today. The rod is awesome, and I have caught so many fish on that rod—it owes me nothing!

## LESSONS LEARNED

I can remember quite clearly one of my many early lessons learned while catching bass on artificial lures. I know there are a lot of stories out there about big fish being taken on the 5½-inch Rebel, well here's another. I was working a productive jetty, one with deep, dark clear water on its sides and a good rip off the front. It was late afternoon and I left the kids to play on the beach while I made my way out to what I considered a great-looking spot just short of the jetty tip.

The sun was setting behind the dunes when I made my cast and then looked back to the beach where I yelled at the kids to stop acting crazy (like kids?). When I looked back toward my plug I saw a humungous swirl behind it. I had no time to react. There was a sudden jerk and my line drew taught in an instant, to the point where I had to hold on for dear life, my drag was locked down tight! The fish was pulling me in a tug-of-war until finally something gave and there was release.

I guess I won the tug-o-war; my 200 pounds to the fish's maybe 40 pounds (wishful imagination)? I thought for sure the fish had broken off. I cranked up the slack expecting to find nothing on the business end, just a broken line, but I was surprised when I saw my lure coming back. It was a wounded soldier returning from battle. I lifted it close to assess the damage and was surprised at what I saw. The plastic lip was totally broken off and gone. Of the two front treble hooks, the front and middle, two of the three hooks were straight, the back hook had a scale hooked right through the center that was the size of a quarter. It would have been my biggest bass to date. My only estimate is that was huge.

I figure it now to have been a high 30- and possibly a low 40-pound fish. That fish haunted my dreams (nightmares?) for years to follow, until it was replaced by bigger sanctifying fish.

The lessons learned that day were many, and they contributed largely to my becoming a competent surfcaster. The lessons that hurt the most are the lessons you remember best. The biggest mistakes of the afternoon were obvious. I never checked my drag. I now try to remember to check my drag every time I head out. I stopped using factory hooks and change my lure hooks to 3X and 4X strong. At the time split ring changes were not an issue because I figured the hook would straighten before the split ring would open. Upon close examination of many of the lures I had in my bag at the time, I noticed that some of the factory hooks on some of the lures were so weak I could almost bend them by hand.

Remember, hardware is a vital link; don't let it be your weak link.

*When working the jetties, a rod capable of bringing a good fish to where you can grab it is imperative. Rocks also call for heavier leader materials. Equipment is everything and not using the right tackle could cost you a good fish. Would losing a good fish be worth the couple of bucks you saved on cheap tackle?*

# 3

# TOPWATER THRILLS: SURFACE LURES

There is a surface lure for nearly every possible situation that you may encounter in the surf. Our wives may not understand it, but we *really do need* a lot of plugs to cover every condition we find while fishing the edge of the beach. What works best on a crisp cool October night in all likelihood won't be the same plug you will use when fishing a gale in September. That's why we need lures like Cotton Cordell Red-Fin swimmers, metal lip swimmers, torpedo-shape "spook" lures, pencil poppers, Polaris poppers and Roberts casting lures. They each have their special time and place to work best.

Surface swimmers are my favorite plug to catch stripers, and I am in good company with a few thousand others who express their love for these great lures. The highly-stimulating visual strikes that come with little warning and a big crash, come like a bolt of lightning. The sight of the brown shape of a big striper rising beneath the plug produces the best kind of suspense.

*Let's face it; there is something beautiful about a bass crashing a surface swimmer. From the first wake that appears behind the lure until the explosion on the take until you see the bass at your feet, the complete cycle makes for great memories.*

Let's take a look at how each one can help in our search for striper strikes.

## COTTON CORDELL RED-FIN

This time-tested lure is a real gem and a novelty of the striper coast. Many, many striper fishermen of today and our recent past claim this lure to be one of the all-time best lures ever produced—that's saying a lot!

The 5½-inch Red-Fin has taken many large cows, but it's the 7-inch offering that I favor, especially when loaded with added weight. An unaltered Red-Fin, fished right out of the box it came in, will always stay on the surface and it is impossible to get it down and keep it down—but this is a good thing! There are times when you need a lure that stays exclusively on top. It gives the appearance of a large wounded fish swimming on the surface, and it leaves behind it a huge V-wake that calls fish in from a long way off.

The altered, or loaded, Red-Fin can be cast a considerable distance and rides just below the surface with a slow side-to-side swim action that is close to perfect. With a sharp jerk of the rod it will dive and swim quickly before returning to its original slow-swimming pace. The jerk will draw strikes from fish following at a distance, and this trick can be used with other plastic swimming plugs besides the Red-Fin.

## WEIGHTING AND LOADNG THE RED-FIN

As if this plug is not good enough to stand alone, add some weight and it becomes all the more valuable in the surfcaster's arsenal. The extra weight adds casting distance to reach fish just out of range. After the plug is loaded it will swim just below the surface in a tantalizing manner with a slow side-to-side sway.

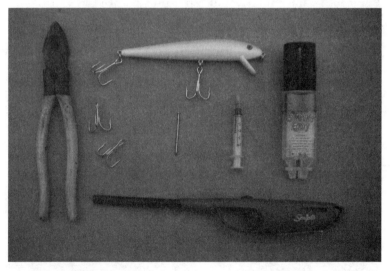

*Materials for loading the Red-Fin. A 6- or 8-penny finishing nail, a heat source, insulated pliers, a syringe and possibly new hooks and epoxy if wanted.*

Loading a 7-inch Red-Fin is a relatively easy task and there are several ways it can be done. Here's how I do it. Hold a 6d or 8d finishing nail with a pair of pliers and heat it over a flame, make sure it is good and hot then push the nail through the top of the lure somewhere towards the front half of the lure, but not on the center seam. The nail will penetrate like a hot knife through butter. You can also drill a small hole with a small drill bit. Then pull out the nail.

You then want to insert 10cc (approximately three table-spoons) of water into the hole. If the lure is transparent you can fill the lure by faucet. Check your water level by holding the lure up to a bright light, fill it to about a ⅜ inch below the middle hook hanger. If it is not transparent a syringe will get the job done. Red-Fins can also be filled with mineral oil or bunker oil.

To fill the hole, simply reheat the nail, and pull some plastic back over the hole with the hot nail. You can also cover the hole with epoxy. If the hole is too big you can reheat the nail and lay some plastic back across the hole, this way the epoxy will have something to grab onto while it covers the span. Once the hole is sealed, hold the lure upside down to make sure it does not leak. Put it into your plug bag and fish it on a regular basis.

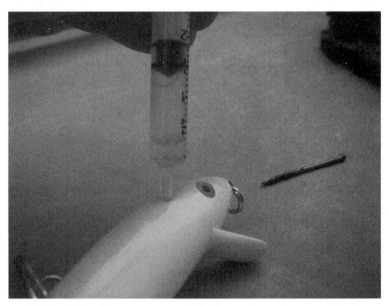

*10 CC (3 tablespoons) of water, mineral oil, your preference, injected with a syringe will do the job.*

Similar plugs from other manufacturers can also be loaded. It is an option that you always have available to you so keep it in mind. Necessity is the mother of invention.

## METAL-LIP SWIMMERS

In recent years, the metal-lip swimmers have become more popular along the striped bass coast and I believe that a lot of the interest is due to the great custom plug builders of today. They make some high-quality plugs with astounding color patterns, but more importantly, they are popular because they are really good at catching fish.

Staples that have stood the test of time include the Gibbs wooden plugs, and I would not be considered crazy if I bet that every surfcaster has at least a couple of Gibb's Danny plugs in their stash. The mass produced Atom-40 and Atom Junior, two longtime heavy hitters, are still good producers today. And let's not forget the famous Creek Chub Pikie, although not as popular today, it's still a great plug. There are many smaller plug builders who put out good workhorse metal-lips today: Big Don, Beach Master, Afterhours, Big Water and R.M. Smith to name a few.

One thing in particular I like about metal lips besides being a proven striped bass producer, and besides the awesome visual hits that they draw, is their size versatility. In my stash I have small wood swimmers that are 2 to 3 inches in length, all the way up to the big-daddy plugs like the

*Metal-lips are not a daytime-only lure, these lures on night tides take a good number of bass.*

Big-Water Pikie, pushing 8 to 10 inches and weighing over 4 ounces. The size difference of local baits calls for different sizes of metal-lip swimmers. For example when mullet are running, throwing a 4- or 5-inch swimmer would work like a charm, but when big bunker are nearby, an 8-inch big wood is the order of the day; remember, big bait catches big fish.

I believe the profile of surface swimmer is critically important. The bass looking up from below sees a wounded baitfish heading for cover. The bass sees this as an easy meal and attacks. The size of the metal lip swimmer should relate directly to the size of the bass available and to the bait present. For example if I was fishing a boulder field in New England I would not chose a small-profile bait because I would anticipate that the big cow bass are migrating and hungry. If I was fishing a quiet back-water or a summer pattern where the big bass are not present, I would offer a smaller profile because I know smaller fish are present.

When working a wood swimmer you want to cast it out and then quickly reel up any slack line so you catch up to it or come in contact with your plug to the point where you feel its resistance against the water. When you are doing it correctly you will feel the pulsating swimming action of the plug transmitted through your rod via the line. Once you make contact you never want to stop until the plug is hanging from the rod tip in front of you. If your lure stops swimming for even a second, it could very well send a suspecting fish off to hunt for something a little more realistic. Staying in touch with the plug throughout the retrieve is critical, and this is one of the main reasons why I fish with braided line.

You also want to control the speed of the swim of your metal-lip plug by not letting it swim, or kick, too fast like when it hits a rip or when a wave pulls back hard on it. At the same time, you also don't want it going too slow or stop either. By keeping it constantly moving with a moderate "kick" you will have success.

I like my metal-lip plugs to stay on or close to the surface. If I want to go deep I will usually use one of the many subsurface swimmers that are available, such as a paddletail, bottle, darter or bucktail, which we'll cover in the next chapter.

There are times and conditions, however, when I want my metal lip to go deep. It is usually where deep pockets and drop-off's accompany good moving current. I also will use it in places where I know big fish that want a big easy meal are likely to hang out. The swimmer will swim deep with the eye turned down and the lip bent up. Adjusting a swimmer is not something you want to do in the middle of the night, so have a couple ready as divers.

In daylight you can watch the lure to be sure that it is swimming perfectly across the surface creating a huge V-wake. It is helpful for you to memorize the feeling of the lure and to remember the rate of retrieve (how fast you are reeling) for optimal plug performance. This way when you fish the same plug in the dark and you can't see it, you can trust that your lure is swimming in a desirable manner.

## IDENTIFYING AND UNDERSTANDING THE LIPS

There are several different lips that are used on metal-lip swimmers, and each lip has a specific purpose. Many plug builders make their own lips for their own style of lure action, and since there are so many variations and combinations of lips and plugs, there is no way they can all be covered specifically. I will attempt to generally organize them so that you will know what to look for next time you are making a purchase or looking for a particular action on a plug that serves a specific purpose. Hopefully this will give you a general idea of what to look for.

The Danny plug is a very popular metal-lip swimmer made with a slow surface retrieve in mind. Its flat nose and relative lack of slant to the head and the wide lip relative to the plug's overall size allows it to stay on the surface and not dip its nose. I like Danny plugs because they wobble and swim leaving a wake on the surface.

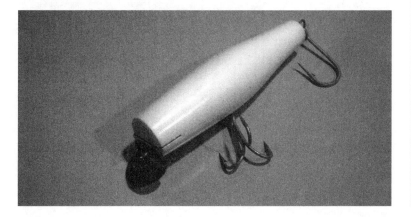

The Pikie swims with a medium wobble created by the small slant on the head that helps it to get that great action. The wide lip gives it a medium swim and also allows for the lure to swim deeper if the retrieve is cranked faster.

The Surfster body is very distinguishable with its humped back and slanted nose. The slant of the head and the spoon-type lip allows this plug to stay on the surface and dip its nose a little. It is used with a slow retrieve.

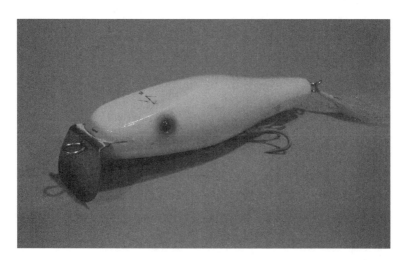

The Atom-40 Style has a more rounded nose and its body is straighter along the sides than the Surfster or Danny. It has a tight wobble. By adjusting the eye and lip this lure can go from surface to diver.

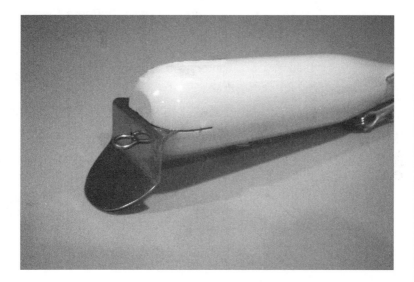

The Lefty-style plug has surfaced in recent years as a commonly made plug that really has its own category. The Lefty lip is smaller and not as wide so it creates a tight fast swim on the plug.

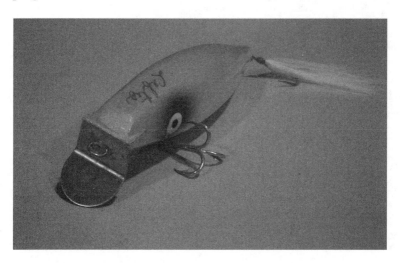

## METAL-LIP ADJUSTMENTS FOR MORE ACTION

There are several ways to adjust the swimming action of a metal-lip swimmer. Bending the eye down slightly will cause the plug to swim higher or on top. Bending the eye up will make it swim deeper and dive. You can also adjust the metal lip; with the lip down the lure will swim shallow on, or just below, the surface, with the lip bent up it will swim deeper with a wider side-to-side swim. (Note: I suggest not touching the lip until you are very sure of what you are doing and why you are doing it).

## STANDARD POPPERS

A workhorse of the surf is the standard popper, the most basic and the easiest popper to use. Creek Chub and Atom poppers are solid plastic which means they both cast well and they sink if you stop retrieving. As a rule I like floating poppers as you can do more with them. Smack-It, Stetzko's Nauset Popper and Tsunami are very good floating poppers.

There is something special about the commotion of a popper that triggers a fish's response, and a violent response it can be! Fish react in-

*My favorite custom-made pencil is made by PlugCaster Lures. The pencil is perfectly weighted for optimal casting and holds up to the rigors of rock and water. This is one of the best pencils on the beach today.*

stinctively and aggressively to these lures, and that's why they catch a lot of striped bass.

I like to work the standard popper by retrieving it with a rhythmic chug. Something along the lines of: jerk-crank three times-jerk-crank three times, and so on. Keeping a good rhythm usually gives the fish time to home-in on the target and then get its timing ready for the strike. You'll need to do some experimenting with most every popper before you can be really good at working them. There are times when this lure will work when no others will. Being good at working poppers is imperative if you want to be good with artificials.

## POLARIS POPPERS

The Gibbs Polaris popper and the Super Strike Little Neck poppers are close to the top on my favorites list, and they are arguably the best poppers ever made. This style popper is one of the great fish-catching lures on the beach, extremely versatile and possessing remarkable cast-ability. It can be popped much the way the standard popper is fished, or it can also be used in a way similar to the pencil popper. It is constructed in such a way that it is multi-faceted. Play around with various retrieve styles and don't be afraid to mix it up when you get into a real-time surf situation.

I fish this lure in many different ways and all of the ways have produced at one time or another. Sometimes I retrieve it with short consecutive strokes while reeling the entire time: pop-pop-pop-pop. Sometime I retrieve it like pop-slosh-crank the reel four times, pop-slosh-crank the reel four, then I shake the rod wildly causing the popper to dance and throw water, somewhat like a pencil popper, and then I go back to a rhythmic cadence again.

My bud Mark Jolliffe swears by his favorite retrieve action that pops and then slides the popper in long slashes across the surface. He feels this action works the best. I have never done well that way, but he does, proving that there are many ways you can work with this plug. Experiment and try to uncover all of its secrets because it has many.

It's important for me to mention that the Super Strike Little Neck 3-ounce popper is my go-to plug when I have wind in my face that is so strong it blows my breathe back down my throat. This thing can cast into a wind like there is no wind at all. I love this plug for that situation. This lure, in the sinking style (black eyes are the sinking models, the green eyes are floaters) can also be retrieved at a medium-speed, steady retrieve so it will ride just below the surface similar to a metal-lip swimmer. Try it, you'll like it. On a calm, fair-weather day this is the lure that can get to fish when they are located far off the beach. Its distance capabilities are amazing.

One thing I never do with this popper, or any popper for that matter, is reel it in as fast as I can, letting it slide and skim across the surface. I see this done quite a bit, but this technique will only draw bluefish strikes.

## PENCIL POPPERS

There is nothing more titillating than watching a bass come up from behind and then take a pencil popper. At times they follow the lure for a short time before the strike, and I call this the triple wake. The lure leaves

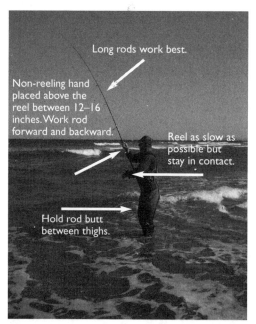

a wake and then you will see two more wakes caused by the dorsal and tail fin of the striped bass. This is the time your heart starts pounding and your adrenaline runs heavy; a time when it's tough to remain calm and composed. There is something about this lure that drives fish wild, and it will often catch striped bass at times when nothing else will.

The secret to your success comes through knowing how to work the pencil. It's the most unusual retrieve technique of all the striper lures. You do this by casting the lure out and then putting the rod butt between your legs just

*Tips for penciling; a long, top-quality rod and some practice will make the pencil popper one of your most effective weapons. Working this lure correctly is what will make this lure produce. A slow wobble on the surface is not the right way to work a pencil.*

north of your knees. As you come tight to the lure after taking up any slack line, hold the rod about 12 to 16 inches above the reel with your right hand, and with this hand you will whip the rod tip forward and backward in a steady rhythm. This will cause the pencil to dance left and right, and to slap the water, throwing spray all around. Your left hand will be reeling, but the trick is to reel as slow as possible while still keeping your line tight enough to keep the pencil dancing.

Whatever you do, once you see the fish and a magnificent strike, don't panic, and for the love of it all, don't stop reeling! Keep a tight line until you feel the weight of the fish then set the hook firmly. Every so often the fish will follow you all the way up to where you are standing. When this happens stop your retrieve briefly and then do several short jerks and twitches to keep the lure moving. Sometimes it is just not meant to be, however, so make another cast and make the lure dance again.

My favorite pencil popper has become the PlugCaster PencilCaster, and I am not saying this because I am on their pro-staff. I really believe in this thing! This plug, made by Rich Karpowicz, is a fine lure, and as with all of his work it is very well engineered. When cast it flies motionless through the air, which is important because when it is wobbling and rolling in flight the distance is greatly compromised. The wobble-free flight also shows you that it is perfectly weighted and balanced. When working this pencil you do not have to bust your groin working this thing as hard as you have to work some others. It does quite well with a simple to-and-fro shake of the rod. I find that this is valuable to me when endurance becomes an issue, like fishing with a pencil over a prolonged period.

The finish also holds up very well. A 4-ounce yellow and redhead pencil I used through most of one spring season caught over 30 big bass, and if you saw the minimal wear on the plug you would never believe it. To me that is a good value!

## GETTING SPOOKED

A simple lure, the freshwater Zara Spook from Heddon has grown bigger and is now a real good striped bass surf lure. Similar plugs have been brought over to the saltwater environment by great plug builders like Afterhours and Big Fish. This style of lure in saltwater is retrieved in much the same way as in freshwater only on a larger scale. The rod tip is pumped so the plug darts and flips with a terrific side-to-side motion that creates a lot of surface splashing and commotion, and it symbolizes a baitfish in distress—another golden opportunity for a hunter striped bass to strike.

You have to practice with this lure too because every plug you try is slightly different. Each one seems to have a learning curve of its own and you have to become familiar with how it works.

## LONG-DISTANCE CHAMPIONS

Lures such as the Robert's Casting Lure and the Line Stretcher are made basically for long-distance casting, which at times is necessary to hit distant fish that are working a football field away. With the Robert's lure you'll need binoculars to see where it lands. I have hit bass on this lure, but I go to it more whenever bluefish hit the happy hunting grounds. They are all made from hard plastic so they are rugged and durable.

*The Surface Crew. Just a few of my favorites, top to bottom: Super Strike's 2⅜-ounce Little Neck Popper, PlugCaster's 2.5-ounce PencilCaster, Smack-It's standard popper, Robert's 3-ounce Ranger, and Afterhour's 2.5-ounce Dook.*

## WHEN TO USE THEM

*Here are some suggestions for what lure you would use in a particular situation.*

**Red-Fin:** Used in calmer water. This is an all-surface plug.

**Loaded Red-Fin:** Used when distance matters and you want to throw a bigger offering for bigger fish. This plug is also a good whitewater plug, it digs well. It casts well into a head wind.

**Metal Lipped Swimmers:** Good plugs for calm to medium water and when medium-size baits like mullet and peanut bunker dominate the scene. I like them while on jetties or in boulder fields.

**Standard Poppers:** These are sometimes the heavier poppers made of solid wood, solid or hollow plastic. When distance matters they are a good option. Also good when bluefish show up. They can be used in all types of conditions. Very good around peanut bunker schools.

**Polaris Poppers:** Good to use just about anytime, anywhere. When you need distance and cutting into or through wind this lure, especially Super Strikes 3-ounce Little Neck is a must-have plug. This is a very good attention getter.

**Pencil Poppers:** Great casting lures when distance matters. Any time is the right time. Use 2-ounce size when smaller baits are present and the 3- to 4-ounce, 9-inch size when the big baits and big bass show up.

**Torpedo-shaped plugs**: Zara-Spook style lures are good almost anytime, I like them in blitz conditions.

**Roberts Casting Lures:** Good for extremely long casts or when bluefish come around.

*Bill Sistad wrestles a lunker to the beach that hit a big Bob Hahn pikie.*

# 4

# SUB-SURFACE SWIMMERS

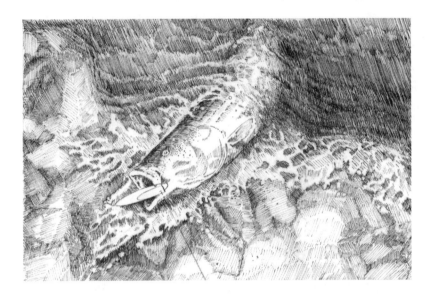

Striped bass don't always strike top-water lures, so the mid-depth area of the water calls for lures that swim below the surface. These sub-surface swimming lures work the water that ranges from just below the surface to just off of the bottom.

Working the mid-column water depth helps you get a lure down a little deeper when the bass are holding close to deep structure and when they show no interest in a surface lure. If the fish are deep in the rocks at the end of a jetty they will look up and see a mid-column offering. If they are higher in the column or near the surface they will still see the lure below them or right in their direct line of vision. This is what you want. The sub-surface swimmer is also an invaluable tool if the bottom terrain is unfriendly, a place with lots of snags and hang-ups. The sub-surface swimmer can be worked so it goes deep, but not so deep as to get hung up.

I also associate sub-surface swimmers with water that "pulls hard" against the lure and fast-moving water. Strong rips, powerful longshore currents and big surf will be a time when you will want to break out some of the sub-surface swimmers. The best places to use them would be in rivers or inlets that have hard- or fast-pulling current, canals, jetty tips, or open beach rips.

The mid-column swimmers are the most difficult to become intimately familiar with because you don't usually get a real good look at them unless you are fishing in super-clean water in daylight. When working surface lures you can watch and learn the action, but this is not always possible with the diving sub-surface lure. It becomes a "feel" thing, so a good surfcaster must learn the feel of a correctly swimming sub-surface plug.

Although you cannot see the action or the depth that the lure is working you can feel when it hits bottom, and that is an indicator as to how deep the plug is working. Here's a trick to get familiar with the water's depth and what the bottom consists of at your spot: attach a sinker to your line, cast it out and let it bounce on the bottom as you retrieve it. This will help you quickly learn what the bottom terrain is like by the feel of the sinker as it scrapes through sand, rocks, mud or shells and where the deeper holes are located. This is another huge advantage of using extra-sensitive braided line.

I like to know exactly what my target area consists of and what each of my plugs will do as I impart action to them. I go out of my way to become familiar with a plug and its swimming action. I've gone so far as putting on a dive mask in the swimming pool while someone reels plugs past me. No, it is not the same as ocean current, but I can get a very clear idea of what to expect. Intimately knowing every nuance of your swimmer is essential to good planning and strategy.

## PLUG MODIFICATION

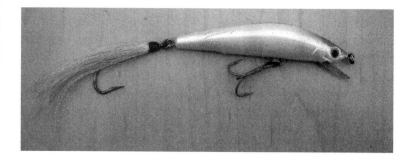

I replace the tail treble hook with a single hook on most of my plugs before they go into the surf bag. The single hook is dressed with bucktail and I have not found any decrease in my hook-ups because of the missing treble. In fact, I believe I get more strikes because the added action of the bucktail makes the lure look livelier.

The rear treble also does more damage to the striped bass, hooking the fish's head in the eye, gills or throat area. A lot of my metal-lips don't even have a hook on the tail end, just a wire dressed with bucktail or feathers. Bass hit the head or front of the lure probably 90 percent of the time anyway so why cause collateral damage to the fish?

I also have a hunch that the single tail hook dressed with white bucktail may draw more strikes especially on the small- to medium-size hard-body plastic swimmers, like the Bomber and Yo-Zuri. The white of the bucktail draws attention because it is easier to spot in dim light. The hard plastic swimmers "kick" a little more than I like so the hair slows down that action just a bit. And that is to my liking.

I also like a single dressed hook on all of my poppers too, especially the bigger ones. I feel the long hairs hold the back of the popper down in the water just a bit and gives the front end of my pencils more freedom from surface tension thus they dance better.

## BOTTLE PLUGS

This plug is also known as the casting swimmer and it's a specialty lure to be used when you need to penetrate the wind and still get good casting distance. When the weather gets to be what the non-fisherman calls bad, but what I call glorious with high surf and hard winds, this plug needs to be considered as one of the first to come out of the bag. The casting swimmer will outcast any metal-lip swimmer or darter in a head wind.

What also makes this plug valuable is its ability to dig and hold in big rolling surf. It is one of my favorite plugs when fishing rough surf with strong current such as beneath the lamp at Montauk and places such as that.

This plug is also a very good choice when fishing in hard-pulling currents like rips, inlets and rivers. It will dig down, stay there and give the bass a good look at a possible meal. The plug can also produce in calmer water and less windy weather, but that is not as common. Big bottle plugs are especially good choices when fishing night tides and they will take their fair share of trophy bass.

The bottle imitates the bigger baits such as squid, snappers (juvenile bluefish), bunker, herring and blackfish. To fish a bottle plug correctly you need to maintain a tight line to the lure. After the cast, crank the reel handle to quickly catch up to your lure, and once you do, give it a good hard jerk or two, which will cause the plug to dig and dive. Once down below the surface, reel only fast enough to keep contact with the plug and to feel its hard pull. The faster you reel the deeper it will dive. You want to let this plug work, so don't force it. If it pulls too hard against the rod and line, slow down your retrieve. If you feel it slowing substantially, increase your retrieve. It's important to stay in contact the entire time.

My favorite bottles are the Gibb's, especially in the 3-ounce size when big bunker and big bass swim close to the beach. Another good choice is the Super Strike Little Neck Swimmer at 2-3/8 ounces. It's a good casting plug and is extremely durable because it's made of solid plastic; a good choice for those times when bluefish seem to crowd the surf and are mixed in with the bass. One of the characteristics that sets the Little Neck swimmer apart from the Gibb's is that it is capable of digging into the water much quicker. It was designed that way to get you into the targeted depth and strike zone. This is very important when you have hard cross wind where your line is getting pulled and bowed in the wind. In this situation you want to keep your rod tip down perhaps even into the water so it is not affected by the wind until you come tight and feel the plug working.

As far as colors go, I have always done well with the all yellow, olive back with white belly and the all black at night.

## DARTERS

The darter is another specialty lure, at least for me, although some will argue vehemently that it is a go-to lure, that argument coming mostly from the eastern tip of Long Island. It does really well in deep, fast-moving current such as in a rip, river or a jetty rip. It is not a good lure for heavy surf or when wind is in your face.

This lure digs once you reel in any slack line and catch up to it. As you reel, the darter swims in a slow side-to-side motion darting left and right, hence its name. It's suspected that the slow side-to-side, unpredictable action makes for an easy big-bass target—an easy meal. This may be why it accounts for a lot of big fish. This lure imitates many of the large baits that swim our surf waters such as herring, bunker, snappers, juvenile weakfish and squid.

While it is usually associated with hard-moving current it can be fished in calmer waters, although there are other lure options that are a better choice than the darter in that situation. Some of the big name darters are Super Strike, Gibb's, Beachmaster and PlugCaster. These are all proven bass catchers, and they all work great, but they do have subtle differences in their actions. You need to experiment with several different darters to discover what they all can do, then fish the one that works best for your local water conditions. Darters work best when you have confidence using them.

I prefer the Super Strike Zig Zag darter. It runs very consistently due to its plastic manufacturing process that gives the lure consistency in weight, something not found in wood. I feel very comfortable with it and I find it very consistent.

I gave Don Musso a call to learn more about the intricacies of this lure—after all, he's the creator of it, and who better to talk to than the originator? We spoke at length about just about all of the Super Strike products. Don gave some very good info and as many others who have spoken to him will attest, he is a man who loves to fish, has a huge body of knowledge and knows exactly what he wants in a lure, especially those lures that he has a hand in making. He is one of the best plug developers of our time and he loves sharing information and talking about lures.

When fishing the Zig Zag, Don suggests that you cast it out, then catch up to the lure by getting the slack out of the line, and then retrieve it at a slow and steady pace. That doesn't sound very intricate does it? It's not. The key is concentrating on feeling the plug as it swims.

If the basic retrieve doesn't work, here are modifications you can try. Don says he will usually throw the darter five to six times and if there's no interest he varies or mixes up the retrieves. His first suggestion is to cast, catch up, then integrate several rod twitches every two to three turns of the reel handle, what he calls short jabs. Another technique is to whack back hard with the rod during the retrieve to cause commotion and to draw attention to the erratic retrieve. The point he makes is that by changing the rod motion and the cranking speed, he can bring out many variations in the retrieve techniques that can get strikes from bass. He likes to try things that are non-conventional and it's a good lesson to remember.

Don also reminded me that darters are not just nighttime lures as some fishermen believe. He has had some very good daytime hits with the darter. He reflected upon a day that he and his partner had in Montauk late in the season when herring made a run past the light. They were into fish in the 20-pound class for over an hour on a white darter.

He mentioned that white and yellow are his favorite standards and are a good place to start, but he also says try the light blue back, pink and white (Super Strike herring color), blue back and silver when herring and snappers are around, yellow when juvenile weakfish are present and all-black Zig Zags at night.

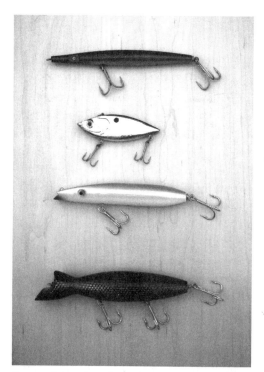

A taste of the sub-surface swimmers. You can't watch them swim once they leave the bag so this is where staying in touch is critical. Top to bottom: Super Strike 2⅜-ounce Super "N" Fish needlefish, Tsunami ¾-ounce Reverb, Super Strike 2⅜-ounce Zig Zag darter and Gibb's 3-ounce Casting Swimmer (bottle plug).

## PLASTIC SWIMMERS

There is a plethora of what I classify as plastic swimmers available today. These could be the most popular lure among the surf contingency all along the striper coast. Their roots run deep in the lore of surfcasting, going back to the days when the first hard-body plastics took the striper coast by storm, like the early Rebel swimmers that replaced the wood Pikies of yesteryear. The plastics did not wear nearly as much as the wooden lures and they cost a lot less.

One of the best advantages when using the plastics is that they are ready to go right out of the package. They need no tweaking and they don't have the inconsistencies of wood. They are hardy and tough, and can take a beating from fish and from being knocked around on jetty rocks and still perform admirably. They are also very easy to use with a minimal learning curve required to figure them out, which in turn makes them popular and likeable.

Although plastics are one of my least favorite lures, I have to reluctantly admit that they do work well and at times are my only option if I want to catch a bass.

Some of the popular age-old names of plastics that are still on the scene today are Bomber, Red-Fin, Rebel and Rapala, (which is actually a wooden plug but it looks just the typical slim plastic swimmer). These old plastics are reliable plugs that have taken good numbers of fish throughout their existence. Plastic plugs are probably the most-fished surf lures of today and are heavily favored by newcomers to the sport.

One of the most popular of this style lure is the Bomber. It comes in various sizes and colors, which increases its fish-catching value. Some of the most commonly used Bomber plugs include the 17A measuring 7 inches and weighing 1½ ounces, the 16A at 6 inches and ⅞ ounce, the A-Salt is 5¾ inches long and weighs 1 ounce, while the ½-ounce 15A is 4¾ inches long. These various sizes and weights give you a good selection of lures from just one lure brand and their uses are wide ranging. Most of the Bombers are also available in jointed-body versions that impart more life and have a little more action.

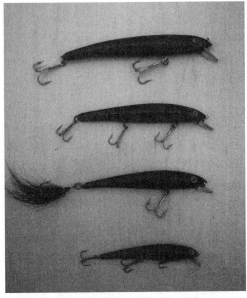

*A long-standing and productive lure, Bombers can provide the entire spectrum in size and color for the surfcaster from the ocean waters to the back bay. Shown here is a good range of sizes; the Long A 7-inch, 16 A 6-inch, A-Salt 5¾-inch (modified) and the 15A 4¾-inch.*

The must-have Bomber colors include yellow, chicken scratch, school bus and black. Other favorite colors that produce bass are the olive/silver, black/purple, baby bluefish, baby striper, black/silver flash and chartreuse.

Bombers cast fairly well and have a great action when retrieved at a slow to medium speed. Throw in an occasional twitch of the rod for good measure.

A relatively new partner to the ranks of hard plastics is Yo-Zuri, a series of hi-tech plugs that are very well engineered. They quickly became my favored hard-plastic swimmer. While the Crystal Minnow is a good producer with its holographic flash and tight life-like swim, it is the Yo-Zuri Mag-Minnow that is my number one plastic swimmer. It casts almost twice as far as the Bomber because the Mag-Minnow has a special magnetic weight transfer system built into it. Internal ball bearings shift from front to back while casting providing a very good load on the rod adding extra distance to the lure.

Another great plug from Yo-Zuri is the Mag Darter, and though this lure wears the name darter, I do not consider this a darter-type plug like the traditional darters mentioned previously. This is a mid-water swimmer and a fabulous bass catcher with a well-deserved reputation. It has the Yo-Zuri Mag technology with the internal magnetic transfer system built-in, which makes it a dynamite caster. For me, it falls into a class of its own because really there is no other like it. The bass just love this lure because its action is slow and deliberate, with a nice side-to-side swimming action.

## THE MIGHTY BUCKTAIL

Oh, boy, much has been written about the timeless bucktail, and rightfully so because it's a great bass lure, so let's take a look at what makes it tick and how we can catch lots of bass with it.

Bucktails are a good choice when you need casting distance and also when you need a lure to penetrate the water column and get right on the bottom. They are responsible for taking a good tally of fish every season, and they are an excellent choice in rivers and inlets and anywhere there is fast-moving water because of their ability to dive and to stay down deep right in the face of big fish.

The action of the bucktail is imparted by the fisherman's wrist and the whip of the rod, and it takes a little practice to get the rhythm down. Once you get it, however, it's like riding a bike, you'll never forget it.

The weight you choose for your bucktail depends on what the water in front of you is doing and how hard it is pulling. For slow-moving water you can begin with ½ to ¾-ounce bucktails, but for fast, deep water you'll need to cast 3 to 6 ounces to get the depth you want and need.

Bucktails imitate almost every bait in the ocean from squid, to shrimp and bunker, so this bad-boy is very versatile. They can be fished just as you would get them at the tackle shop (undressed), but I feel they are more productive when they are dressed with an Uncle Josh's #70 pork rind in white, or a plastic 6-inch Mr. Twister tail.

## THE MAGIC OF NEEDLEFISH

The needlefish could very well be the most versatile lure available to the surfcaster today because it can be fished in so many different ways. It can be worked on the surface similar to a pencil popper, it can be reeled at a moderate pace across the surface, it can be allowed to sink toward the bottom using the countdown method and then retrieved dead slow. The lure amazes me because it holds numerous "mysteries of retrieval" that you will need to personally uncover as you fish it.

Talk to other surfcasters, read about various retrievals and speed rates, and then try them all, always experimenting until you find one or two that work for you in your own fishing situations. What may work at Montauk may not work so well on the Cape. What works on a south wind may not work the same on a northeast wind. I don't think there is a right or wrong way, just many ways that produce fish for you—they're all right!

I find it interesting that as I meet different bass men in my travels along the coast, it seems that each one has a different way to fish the needlefish plug and each person swears that his way is correct and "guaranteed" to catch fish. Could this be? It's fun try them all.

The needlefish also comes in various sizes and weights and imitates a wide spectrum of bait, ranging from the small Spofford and Boone needlefish plugs all the way up to Afterhours 10-incher weighing more than 4 ounces. The short and stubby needlefish plugs are also good for those times when a big lure won't catch, especially when the local bait is small. The beautiful thing about the needle is that it can be fished in any part of the water column, from the surface down to the bottom, wherever the bait and bass may be holding.

*Needlefish could be the most versatile lure in the surf, ranging in all sizes and shapes. A few shown here top to bottom: Afterhours 10-inch, 4-ounce; Super Strike Super "N" Fish needlefish in 1 ounce (modified), Hab's Stubby needle, Hab's 2-ounce needle and Jolliffe's 3-ounce (modified) needle.*

I was fishing Montauk one afternoon when I foul hooked something peculiar. It wasn't a striper or blue, and it put up a bit of a fight. I wondered what I had and hoped that whatever it was it would stay on the hook so I could see it. Much to my surprise it was a real needlefish. A long skinny fish, about 10 inches long with a body similar to a freshwater gar. It was silver in color with long narrow jaws. A lot of things came to light for me at that moment when I saw this fish. I could then see where and why skinny lures such as pencil poppers and needlefish were effective. The needlefish, despite its profile, imitates many different fish. Some think that it should be used only when sand eels are in the neighborhood, but this is in no way true.

For this lure to be effective for you, you need to work with it and you need to become intimate with it and by doing so your confidence in it will grow especially once you start banging some fish. It is one of the harder lures to trust because you can't ever get a good feel for the lure. It has little water resistance, unlike the metal-lip swimmer that has plenty of pull. With a needlefish, you simply feel a slight heaviness during the retrieve, and this is what you need to concentrate on and become familiar with.

The basic retrieve for fishing a needle would be to cast, let it sink to the bottom then reel it in dead slow. The late John Haberek, creator of one of the best needlefish ever built, used to say that you need to fish it slooooow. If you are bored you are reeling too fast. Another suggestion he mentioned was that while retrieving it at a moderate pace along the surface, he suggested that I should stop, let it sink down and hit bottom, and then retrieve it again quickly. Well what do you know I tried it one night when the usual retrieves weren't producing and Bingo! It worked.

Another way the needle is used when the bottom is sand, not rock, is to cast it out let it sink to the bottom and then just keep twitching it. This causes puffs of sand, looking like a sand eel coming out of hiding. There is no need for speed with the needlefish retrieve, keep that in mind.

The countdown is a technique where you cast out and count the seconds before you begin your retrieve. The first time you may count to five, the next time 10, and by doing this you are covering all levels of the water column. Working the needlefish at a moderate retrieve with an occasional twitch is a technique that has produced well for me at times.

Don't be hesitant to put a teaser on in front of your needlefish for some added enhancement and to increase your chances.

In my previous book, *The Surfcaster's Guide to the Striper Coast,* I mention the different makes of needlefish and how each is worked according to needle-master Dennis Zambrotta of Newport, Rhode Island. Dennis covers some good stuff, so it's worth repeating.

*Needlefish are very versatile plugs and it would be a mistake to set "hard and fast" rules on how to fish them. Just as in any type of surf fishing there are so many variables involved that may affect your decision on which needlefish to use. They include water depth, water clarity, current, surf conditions, time of year, type of bait present, wind speed and direction, etc. How I use needlefish on the Cape doesn't necessarily work when I'm casting on Block Island. What works when the wind is screaming onshore may not work in flat water (or maybe it will). So, I have my "preferred" methods of using needlefish for every location I fish, depending on the conditions. But I always tell those who will listen to my general rules that bass don't read—so be flexible in your methods.*

*For example—I don't know how many times I've heard casters say they won't cast a needlefish because there are no sand eels around—big mistake. Needlefish plugs can be extremely effective even when there isn't a sand eel on the beach for miles. They can work when the forage is squid, bunker, silversides, whatever.*

*A big key when using needlefish plugs is confidence. Once you get over the fact that a needlefish plug doesn't need to do a lot in the water (as in "wiggle") you will gain confidence. Fish it high or low, night or day, light or dark pattern, they all work when the time is right and it's up to the caster to figure that out.*

*Another key is being versatile—being versatile and adapting to changing environments on the beach while casting needlefish will allow you to uncover the mysteries of the plug. After all, isn't learning the most satisfying part of surf casting? It is to me.*

*I fish many needlefish brands and they all catch at certain times. I personally witnessed the effectiveness of the large size Stetzko Pink Needle in the hands of its creator. I went through my bag of needles trying to duplicate his success—the closest I came was with the Gag's 9" Copper Needle—but Tony still smoked me that particular night with his own creation. Was it the type of needlefish or the fisherman using it? Nothing wrong with being humbled by Tony Stetzko, I'm just one of many in that club.*

*Just remember, success is relative and everyone has their own opinions based on their experiences. Others may tell you different and it would behoove any surf caster to pay attention to other opinions. Now you have some of my general rules for using various needlefish plugs and all that I mention have a great track record for taking trophy stripers from the beach.*

Some of the big name needlefish lures are made by Super Strike, Gibb's, Gag's, Afterhours, and I would also mention the Hab needlefish but since his untimely passing I think a lot of his needles will become more keepsakes than workhorses. I would guess that he would rather we fish them than save them but it is of course a very sensitive issue and one of personal choice.

## NOISY RAT-L-TRAPS

The Rat-L-Trap has been around for many years and I used it regularly for catching weakfish off the Manasquan Inlet's north jetty back in the late 1980s. Its slender, thin body with its football-shape profile gives it the look of a peanut bunker, a favorite food of the striped bass. When I used it for weakfish, it was to imitate spot, a local baitfish, which were in good numbers at the time, as were the weakfish.

Trap-style lures are weighted so they cast very well and they also sink quickly. The quick sink for me makes this a specialty lure, one that is used in specific conditions or situations. I don't throw it much from the beach, but it is very good in fast moving water where it gets right down into the fish's line of vision while being swept by the current. It is also good for a hard-pulling jetty rip where penetration to the depths is vital.

While the weight makes this lure valuable, the internal rattle puts it over the top. This thing is noisy! When throwing it at night in dark waters that are pulling strongly I can trust the rattle is working its magic and this gives an added element that helps fish find the lure and home in on it.

One thing to remember before throwing this lure to powerful stripers, especially a freshwater-size version, is that you will need to check and possibly replace the split rings and factory hooks with something substantially stronger like heavy-duty split rings and VMC hooks.

Some of the best Rat-L-Trap-style lures on the market are Tsunami's Reverb, Stillwater's Clatter Shad and the original Bill Lewis Rat-L-Trap. Tsunami's Reverb is hard to beat for surf fishing and it is a favorite of many surfcasters.

## TEASING WITH TEASERS

I am sure that you have thought about this, I think every bass hunter has; what is it about a big fish chasing a smaller fish that drives bass crazy. If a snapper is chasing a rainfish, why would a bass butt in and eat the rainfish when the much bigger snapper is right there? "The bass obviously wanted to eat the small fish before the big fish," you say. Do you think the bass wanted an appetizer before the main meal? In the highly competitive world that stripers live in, where they compete viciously with each other for food, I doubt that to be true. So why is it that the bass hits the teaser and forgoes the big delight? All I can say is, "Who knows?" Certainly not me, but I don't really care. So long as it is a productive means of catching fish I will use teasers.

In all likelihood when the bass are keying in strictly on very small baits, this is the time they will hit the teaser. I saw this happen one October day in Montauk. When the waves would crest you could see oodles of bass and shoals of rainfish all through the waves. The bass would not take any plug offering that anyone would cast to them. Finally someone had the notion to try a ¼-ounce pink bucktail and sure enough that is what they wanted. That guy was the only one who caught bass—and he got about 20 of them! Go figure. I wasn't carrying any bucktails that small and honestly don't know if I even owned one before that day, especially in pink, but I sure do now.

*The smallest offering that the surfster throws could be the most productive. This small bass found a teaser to its liking. Teasers work well when small, thin-profile baits are present.*

One of the truly powerful weapons of the mighty surfcaster is the smallest, the little teaser, and as I just mentioned above, little things can produce big results. The teaser is the bonus persuader. At times it is the primary lure and at other times it is the secondary persuader, but either way it needs to be considered every time you fish with artificials. It is productive when small or thin-profiled bait are present such as bay anchovies (rainfish or whitebait), juvenile spearing and small sand eels. There are many different types and colors and shapes of teasers, so you can easily find one that matches the small baits that are present.

# 5
# THE RUBBER REVOLUTION

With progress comes technology, with technology comes a better way to catch bass. The latest technologies introduced a new wave of soft-plastic lures, called "rubber" baits by many surfcasters. Actually they aren't rubber at all, but are made of soft plastic that feels rubbery, hence the nickname.

The paddletail shad could arguably be considered the best new lure to rise through the ranks since the Bomber hit the surf. The Lunker City Slug-Go is another lure that has proven its worth by the number of big fish it has taken along the beaches in recent years.

The plastics used in today's rubber surf lures are strong yet soft, and by adding special detailed coloring and spray-on paints, you have imitators of baits that are simply astounding. They are so lifelike and produce so well that it is sometimes a tough decision to turn to one of the older standby lures that we grew up using.

I believe that the rubber lure's biggest asset is its softness. When a fish hits a hard-plastic or wood plug, it knows immediately that something is awry because baitfish are not hard, they're soft. When a bass rolls and smacks a plug it feels something strange and may hesitate, or be deterred, whereas with the soft-rubber baits they will "trust" it longer, keep it in their mouths a bit longer thereby giving you, on the other end of the line, some extra time to react and an extra split second to set the hook. This small amount of extra time means more fish for you.

Equally important, the lifelike soft body has so much flexibility the rubbers swim with lifelike realism. To see one swim is almost like watching a fish swim. On one of my first days of swimming a rubber shad I recall looking into the water behind my lure and seeing a school of peanut bunker following it. Somehow between the moment my lure hit the water and sometime during the retrieve, this school of 'nuts voted my old boy the leader of the pack, and I was mightily impressed by this foolery. If my shad could lead the real, live-bait parade it could and would surely fool the bass or other hungry predators nearby. Thus a big check-

*The paddletail shad has risen to prominence among the surf contingency. Its natural swimming action, soft body and ability to be used almost anywhere in any condition makes it a go-to lure when plying the skinny waters.*

mark was penciled in my confidence column for that lure. Its effectiveness was obvious.

The one shortcoming of the rubber lures is teeth. No they don't bite you, but the bluefish bite them. Once the blues enter the scene the rubbers go bye-bye either by their own choice as bluefish chop them up, or by your choice to save your lures and put them back in the surf bag where they are safe. If you are throwing a paddletail and a blue bites off the tail at the hook there are probably a million things that you could get madder at; but when a blue takes the tail off a Slug-Go that you took 15 minutes to rig, it can be quite a bit agitating.

## SWIM SHADS

Whether you call them swimbaits, swim shads or paddletail shads, these are one of my favorite types of lures because they can do a lot of things very well. They are versatile and attract striped bass like a magnet, very good characteristics that you would look for in an artificial. By versatile I mean this lure can be fished on a calm bluebird day or in a stiff northeaster. This bad boy can go anywhere. I would have no problem throwing this on a calm night, or from a jetty, in the rips at Sandy Hook, or into the teeth of a northeast gale at Montauk. It is one of the few lures that transcends all conditions.

The lifelike appeal of swim baits is incredible. Let me tell you about a day at Fisherman's Supply, a tackle shop in Point Pleasant Beach, New Jersey, near where I live. It has a floating dock out back where Ron, the store keeper and local surf guru, takes new or prospective plugs and swims them to see just how good they are, and if they are "store-worthy." He also takes surf rats down there to show them the action on a new plug that he is trying to sell them (good businessman).

Every once in a while I walk into the store and Ronnie will say "Come on down to the dock. I just got some new plugs in. Let's go swim these and check out the action!" He'd have a small cardboard box of about 10 to 20 plugs of all makes and models. I have never been one to turn down a good plug-swimming demonstration so one day we go down to the dock, which is about 30 feet long protruding out into the water, and Ron throws out a plug and retrieves it along the dock while I stand further out and watch it swim by. It's a pretty cool thing to get such a good look as it swims. Then Ronnie says, "Hey check out this new 10-inch Storm Kickin' Minnow." He casts out and retrieves it, and I watch it come out of the deep channel waters. It swims by and looks very lifelike with a nice natural "S" pattern, very enticing. "Hey look!" I said, "Isn't that neat, there's a couple of small baitfish following the lure!" Then as the lure swam past me I noticed that what I saw wasn't a school of small baitfish following the rubber at all, but rather it was a few spots on the nose of a very large striper. I started gagging and pointing down trying to talk words, but nothing came out, only sounds. Ron says, "What's wrong?" Then he finally saw the big bass following the lure.

That bass followed the lure right up to where he could not retrieve anymore. Ron was laughing and shaking his head in disbelief, and then the bass turned and slowly swam back into the deeper waters of the river from where it came. We both stood with our jaws ajar, giggling like a couple of kids.

Now I don't know if that was a battery-operated remote-control bass that Ron and the store had set up under the dock, but you can be sure that my wallet was open at the cash register a little while later buying several of those Storm rubbers.

If that big striper following the lure wasn't enough to convince even the biggest Doubting Thomas of the effectiveness of the rubber baits, then there is absolutely nothing that can.

Along with the paddletail shad's ability to look lifelike, as if that isn't enough, it also casts like a dream and has the ability to penetrate the water column to any depth. The total package is a terrific lure.

There are at least four rubber paddletail shad producers on the market today; Tsunami, Storm, Calcutta and Panther Martin. Panther Martin was my first introduction to the paddletail shad, but the Tsunami Swim Shad is the one I personally have put all my faith in because it can do whatever I require of it. I have caught an ungodly amount of fish on these shads, and the intricacies of this lure gives it the upper edge over Storm and Calcutta.

The Calcutta Flashfoil Swim Shad's strong points are the colorings and natural shape; these are a dead ringer for many types of local baitfish, but primarily mullet or herring. The problem I find is that the wide body causes it to ride up high in the water column when current is prominent. I do most of my fishing in current, thus the Calcutta gets put in the back seat.

Joining it in the back seat is the Storm Wild Eye which is still a great paddletail, but which I don't favor only because I am not particularly crazy about its hook position. It sits up and out of the body just a little too much for my liking, which I feel costs me fish.

## LET'S FISH 'EM

To get the most potential from a shad, allow it to dive for a few seconds before beginning your retrieve. This lure is best when retrieved at mid-speed, but the rate of retrieve really is contingent on the water movement in front of you. I like to work the shad from bottom to mid-column, down in the zone.

If the water is not pulling hard then a slightly faster retrieve is most effective. Mix in an occasional twitch or a rise-and-fall

*Soft-body baits at night are great bass catchers. Here Crazy Alberto sports a mid-night 20 pounder. To think that it is a daytime-only lure is cutting its potential in half.*

action where you simply pull back on the rod during the retrieve, lifting the shad in the water column and then releasing it to fall back down. This motion will attract fish and break the monotonous uneventful straight retrieve.

When there is faster moving water you should reel much slower, sometimes even stopping the lure completely and work it by just lifting and dropping the rod tip to make the lure flutter in the rip. This all goes back to touch and contact. When you feel the lure pulling hard, you know it's in the center of the rip and it will either stay there or swim itself off into the slower water to the side, which is the water that the bass like to feed in.

Every so often you will be fishing a shad and along comes a school of bluefish mixed in with the bass. Well, you know what happens to your shad right? Yep, chop! You reel in to find it bit off right behind the hook.

Usually you take the shad off and begrudgingly throw it into your plug bag or at somebody (only kidding) while scanning your bag for something that stands up to teeth.

Sometimes a half shad may still work. One day I was aggravated when half a shad came back while in the midst of a combination blues-and-bass assault. I thought about it for a minute and then cast the rubber half bait out again, only this time I let it sink and retrieved it by lifting and dropping the lure very gently with just enough speed to keep contact with the chopped-off lure. I thought if bluefish were attacking and chomping baitfish in half in a feeding frenzy, then in all likelihood the striped bass would be below the blues getting their food the easy way. Sure enough I had two bass on the next three casts fishing with just the head of a rubber shad. I honestly wasn't that surprised.

Another nice thing about the shads is their variety of sizes. They come in everything from 1 inch all the way up to 10 inches. I used to fish the small 1- and 2-inch shads under a local bridge for small bass, blues and weakfish when my kids were small. At the other extreme, throw the 9- and 10-inch shads when the big bunker, shad and herring are getting chased by mama-jama bass.

*Herb Reed's 9-inch rigged Slug-Go is about as close as you can get to a sure thing when bass swim nearby. This 20-pound class fish liked it.*

At night I often like a dark lure, you know, all black, so one small modification I make to the Tsunami paddletail is to break out the old reliable Sharpie marker and go to town. Make sure you allow for drying time because it takes a while for the ink to dry. Once blackened you have an effective night lure.

## THE REMARKABLE SLUG-GO

I hold the 9-inch Lunker City Slug-Go in very high regard based on its ability to catch striped bass. If there are bass in front of me, this lure will catch them. I feel extremely confident with that statement, and that's why the Slug-Go ranks very close to the top of my artificial go-to list. While some think this bait only imitates an eel, I believe that the Slug-Go and similar offerings from Hogy, Bass Candy and Rozi imitate a much wider range of thin-profile baits such as spearing, needlefish and alewife. When it's hungry, I believe a bass will hit any well-presented offering regardless of season or other bait present, so throwing a black Slug-Go at night, anywhere along the striper coast will take bass. This lure has no geographical limit, much like the eel.

The "McKenna Style" Slug-Go is rigged with two hooks and has weights inserted into the body to give it extra weight for casting and balance. It is cast out and then retrieved at a fairly quick pace. My rule of thumb is to reel it as fast as you can without having it break the surface of the water. Intermittent twitches throughout the entire retrieve gives this lure an incredible darting action. The speed and action of the Slug-Go results in quick and powerful strikes from bass. When presented at a fast pace, the bass have very little time to consider it, and since they don't get a good look at the lure, this leads to an impulse strike. I believe this is the strong point of this lure.

### HOW-TO RIG THE NINE INCH SLUG-GO

In *The Surfcaster's Guide to the Striper Coast* I included instructions on to how to rig the Slug-Go, but to make this book the most comprehensive and complete guide for the surfcaster, I have included it here as well, along with some new modifications.

**Materials needed:** 9-inch Slug-Go bodies, 3/16-ounce nail weights, 10-inch rigging needle, 50-pound test Dacron, 7/0 Gamakatsu Octopus hooks, Zap-a-Gap glue.

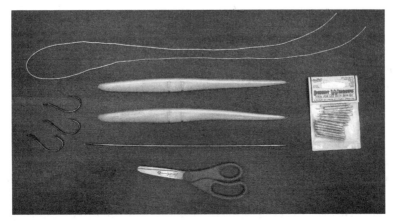

**STEP ONE:** Begin by threading the needle with a 24-inch length of Dacron, then tie off the tag ends with an overhand knot. Pull the Dacron to where the knot is beside the eye. On the opposite end tie on a 7/0 hook with a barrel knot. To tie a barrel knot slide the loop through the eye of the hook, bring it out the open loop, give it a half twist and then put the loop back over the bend of the hook. Repeat this two more times then pull tight; you will then have before you a barrel knot. A Palomar knot will also work.

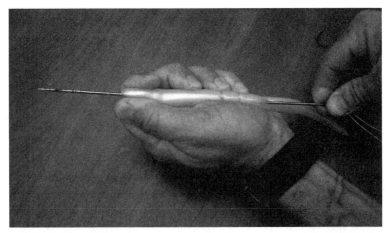

**STEP TWO:** Stick the needle into the bottom of the Slug-Go about ¾ inch behind the jointed section. Push the rigging needle through the center of the Slug-Go. **It is very important to keep the needle in the center of the Slug-Go.** I do this strictly by feeling the needle as it passes through the plastic making sure that it doesn't ever come close to the outside edge, especially at the jointed area. Exit the needle right through the front of the head (mouth). Pull the Dacron and the hook up tight into the body. Cut the needle from the Dacron close to the knot. Your rear hook is now set in place.

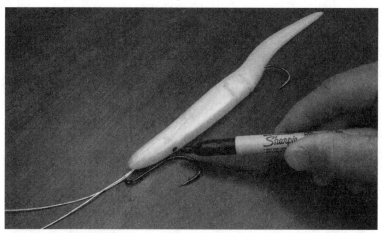

**STEP THREE:** Now you have to attach the front hook. What I like to do is lay the front hook on the outside of the Slug-Go so I know where it will exit on the bottom of the lure body. I then mark it with a Sharpie or put a small nick in the lure with the hook point to show where the front hook will exit. I then run the front hook in through the nose of the bait and out the bottom where I marked it. Again, it is very important to keep the hook centered best as is possible. Your hook will be passing very close to the Dacron that is already there from the rear hook. If you catch it you will feel it, back your hook up and try again. Once you get it where you want it, pull the Slug-Go into place with only the eye of the hook showing. Make sure it is perfect.

Next, pull the front of the Slug-Go back down to the bend of the front hook. You will have before you the two tag ends from the rear hook. Tie these two ends together with a simple overhand knot and then tie about seven half hitches along the hook shank. Tie it off with two overhand knots. Trim off the ends and then glue the entire knot section with Zap-A-Gap. Put the lure aside and let the glue dry.

After the glue dries, do a practice run of sliding the Slug-Go back up to its final resting place just short of the eye of the hook. Make sure everything looks good and is lined up straight. When it looks good, again pull the Slug-Go back down exposing the knot section, glue it again and quickly slide the Slug-Go up to the eye. The glue grabs quickly so do this fast. Look it over to make sure it is straight, and let dry.

**STEP FOUR:** The last step balances the lure with the nail weights. Insert two weights into the front section, running from rear to front and then one directly into the tip of the tail. If you desire additional weight, you may want to add one more weight to the front belly beneath the hook shaft. Once this is done the Slug-Go is ready for business.

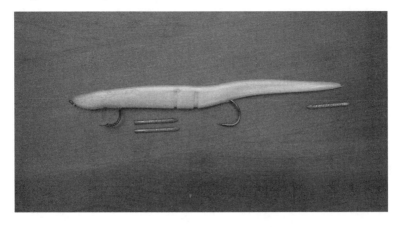

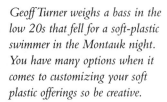

*Geoff Turner weighs a bass in the low 20s that fell for a soft-plastic swimmer in the Montauk night. You have many options when it comes to customizing your soft plastic offerings so be creative.*

## LEADHEADS AND SOFT BODIED PLASTICS

If I said that there were probably at least a few hundred leadhead jig and soft-plastic combinations I probably wouldn't be far from the truth. This particular union gives you a lot of flexibility to develop a bus load of combinations that can be deadly when targeting bass.

When you mix lead and plastic you have an effective, lifelike offering that will go anywhere you want in the water column. One combination that will probably work anywhere in the fishing world for *any* fish is the leadhead and twister-tail combination. Bass love this combo, and I often wonder why it is not used more by other surfcasters—especially me. I have seen it work effectively so many times all along the striper coast that you would think my surf bag would be loaded with leadheads and twister tails, but, no, it's not. I suppose it lacks the romance and excitement of a metal-lip swimmer or a pencil popper.

The most common soft-plastic baits include the shad-body style, Fin-S-type body, worm, twister tail, sand eels or rubbers that look like skinny eels. I don't particularly like to toot one company's horn, but Lunker City has quite a variety of soft plastic baits in many shapes, sizes and colors as

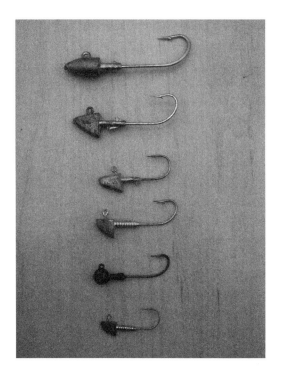

*The shapes and sizes of lead-
heads available today are
amazing. In the surf you can
try anything that you may
think works. Kalin's and
Lunker City make two of
my favorite leadheads.*

well as leadheads available for any type of fishing. If you come up with
an idea for a color you'd like to test out in your local secret spot, Lunker
City's website would be a good place to go brainstorming (*www.lunk-
ercity.com*) because you can see every color they offer. When you come up
with ideas or strategies and need to put pieces together to make it happen, this is a good way to do that. Just because it hasn't been tried before
doesn't mean your idea won't work.

For example, in the Slug-Go/eel category I thought that I really
wanted an eel-type lure in the standard black, but also with a lot of silver and blue flash to imitate the reverse eel skin and to pick up any possible ambient light on a pitch black night. When I searched the Lunker
City site for that specific color, much to my surprise I found a color very
close to what I had in mind for my next Slug-Go rigging. That color is
Blue Ice. I got it, fished it and had moderate success with it. I did not
crush the bass with it, but I did fair. It quenched my desire to try out my
ideas—and it worked! Next year I may try another color combination always searching for that elusive "magic" lure.

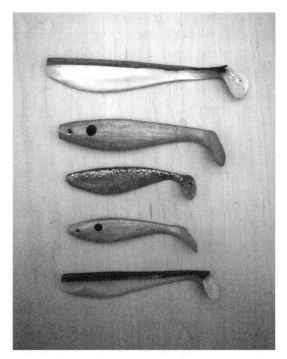

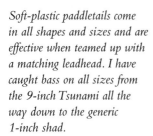

*Soft-plastic paddletails come in all shapes and sizes and are effective when teamed up with a matching leadhead. I have caught bass on all sizes from the 9-inch Tsunami all the way down to the generic 1-inch shad.*

Another unmistakable soft plastic on the market is Berkley's Saltwater Gulp! and Saltwater Power Bait. The Berkley Gulp! baits are made from natural ingredients that release 400 times more scent than plastic baits, and they are infused with scent that all gamefish find indubitably edible. At times, they out-fish everything, including live or natural baits. There are several Gulp! baits that are perfect for striped bass like the sand crab/flea, shrimp, peeler (shedder) crab, shad, clam, pogy (bunker), sandworm, squid, eels, minnow (thin profile) and swimming minnow. Visit their website (*www.berkley-fishing.com*) to get the entire picture of your options.

## LEADHEAD CHOICES

Once you have your soft-plastic body picked out you then need to add a matching and compatible leadhead. For surfside surfcasters looking for the appropriate size leadhead, start at around 1 ounce and work your way toward heavier heads until you find what you need for optimal casting distance and for depth in the water column. For bays and estuaries, slower moving water and smaller fish, you may want to start with a ½-ounce leadhead and work your way up until you find what works. In one of my favorite river spots for example, I use a ¾-ounce leadhead with a 6-inch Mister Twister tail and do quite well.

Leadheads come in many shapes, sizes and weights, which all adds to the versatility of this lure. The most common leadheads are round, bullet, shad head and Fin-S head. There are numerous variations of these basic shapes that can be used in the surf or when wading quiet back waters—even floating heads made of plastic or Styrofoam that look like a leadhead.

The round leadhead is a universal shape and is a good bet to start with. Just be very sure that the hooks on your leadheads are strong enough for the saltwater environs. Some hooks are just rubbish, a paper clip would be stronger. One of my favorite jigheads is made by Kalins; this is a great saltwater jighead. Their hooks are very strong and the hooks are big enough for big saltwater fish. Some jig makers use undersize hooks when they make their jigs, or use fine-wire hooks, and both straighten easily, a definite turn-off for me.

## WORKING THE LURE

The retrieve when fishing a leadhead and soft body varies greatly, as does every situation or location that we fish. You can best get the feel for the retrieve you want by simply watching what your lure does if you work it a few feet off the rod tip and swim it in front of you. Play around while wading in shallow water or off a dock. Try different retrieves to impart life into the jig. Make it dart and dance. See how it looks when jigged, and at fast or slow speeds. Once you have a retrieve that looks like something a fish would eat it, you've got something! Let me say it again; "Know your lures intimately."

Sometimes a straight retrieve is all you will need. The reel-lift-drop-reel sequence also works very well at times. The bass may strike on the lift or sometimes on the drop, and sometimes on the straight retrieve. Be in tune and stay focused when the hit comes to help figure out the pattern for the day. Another good retrieve is the reel-sharp jerk/twitch-reel-sharp jerk/twitch. Try them all and make up your own. I have offered you several, but there are many more so use the process of elimination to filter through retrieves until you find those that work best for you.

Leadhead/soft-body combination lures are great in fast moving current and inlets because they cast very well and penetrate quickly. Keep a supply of various sizes and weights of leadheads when fishing fast moving water. You have to have your offering deep, on the bottom, because that is where the big fish hold. They sit on the bottom of inlets and rivers in a hole or behind structure and wait for the bait (dinner) to come to them. Start with a weight such as 1½ ounces; if you don't feel it bouncing on the bottom, go heavier by a half ounce. Keep changing until you

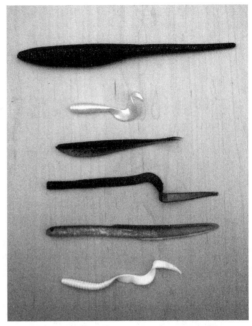

*Soft-body plastics come in all shapes and sizes. There is no excuse that you can't find a lure to match the hatch.*

have what you want. As the conditions and tides change, so does the flow. Stay "in touch" with your lure, know what is going on . . . concentrate!

## TEASING WITH TEASERS

Small soft-plastics also make great teasers. Among the most popular are 2- and 3-inch shads, grubtails, twister tails and slender Fin-S jerk baits. Other good choices include the 4-inch Tsunami Halo-eels, which take a good share of fish along the beaches. They are a great alternative choice instead of feather or hair teasers. They can be rigged on the Mustad O'Shaughnessy 3407DT in sizes from 1/0 to 4/0.

## GLUE IS GOOD

Whenever you slide a plastic tail onto a teaser hook or a leadhead you should always finish the deal with a drop of adhesive. This keeps the soft-

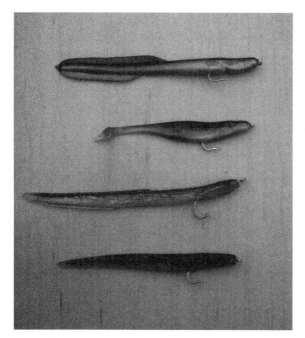

*The soft plastics also make great teasers, small is not all bad. Top to bottom; 4-inch Alou eel, Gotcha 4-inch Trout Killer, Tsunami 4-inch Holographic eel and Lunker City 4-inch Fin-S Fish. Take your pick, you can't go wrong.*

plastic teaser in place during repeated casting and retrieving, and also makes it harder for a short-striking fish to pull the plastic tail down the hook. I like Zap-A-Gap, a cyanoacrylate (CA) glue commonly called a super glue. It's made by Super Glue Corporation but there are others on the market. Having a small container of this stuff is a must for any surf-caster. Not only is it good for securing plastics to the hook, but also great for sealing knots when rigging. Just remember, this glue sets up and dries extremely fast, within seconds, so know where you are going to position your plastic before you apply the glue and use the glue sparingly, it is very strong.

For those of you who are like me, you will also want to get the Z-7 Debonder from the same company. When you glue your fingers together, you will not need your wife or buddy to cut them apart, which my wife has done for me numerous times while I'm rigging Slug-Gos.

Don't be afraid to experiment with leadheads and soft plastics, your options are endless!

# 6

# TIN SQUIDS AND METALS

"My rod was equipped with a Belmar squid, so I wasted no time in meditation over what manner of fish had attracted my brother fishermen, the gulls, but made my cast, working the lure rapidly shoreward. No strike rewarded my efforts, so again I cast, and yet again without result. And still the gulls darted, swooped, and clamored, as though encouraging me to further my efforts. On my eighth or tenth cast I varied my system, and on the chance that the fish, whatever they were, might be cutting into the bait from below, I allowed the squid to sink, and brought it to me with long, jerky movements. Scarce had I taken a dozen turns when there came a mighty strike which swept the tip of my rod downward, the reel handle striking my knuckle a sound crack as it was jerked from my grasp. Out and out my line swept, while with every nerve a tingle I pressed hard on the leather drag and braced back against the rod. A hundred, two hundred, three hundred feet of line the fish took ere he halted his rush, and swam parallel to the beach. I felt sure that another besides a blue, or else a monster specimen of this hard-fighting species had fastened to my squid, and I played him carefully. Fifteen or twenty minutes of battle he gave *me ere I had him close inshore, and then as he lifted into a curling breaker, with the sun shining greenly through, I made him out. A good striped bass he was, and long before I had succeeded in coaxing him into a wave which laid him gently at my feet I had raised such a to-do that my two friends, aroused at last from their slumbers, joined me, a bit shy as to clothing but fully equipped with rods and tackle.*

*Five bass, ranging up to eighteen pounds in weight, we took from this school in a space of an hour, and then the fish moved onward, and the gulls with them, and we returned to camp for a belated though doubly relished breakfast."*

—Van Campen Heilner, from *The Call of the Surf*, 1920

M etal lures, once known as tin squids, squids or tins, today are simply called metals by surfcasters, and have been used in the surf longer than any other artificial lure that we still use in the surf. Today's lures are not usually made of tin, although some still are, but even that old nickname hangs on as many beach fishermen refer to any metal lure as a tin.

It is obvious that Heilner found the tin squid to be an excellent go-to lure back in the early 1900s. Not only did he often mention tins as his primary artificial lure but he also mentioned various sizes and weights of the tins. Heilner even mentions the effectiveness of tins at night. Other than tins, most of the fishing back in the early days was done with baited hook, but Heilner preferred to take fish on artificials whenever possible. I can't imagine having a tin as my only artificial lure!

Throughout his book *Fishing the Surf,* published in 1941, Raymond Camp speaks regularly about the use of metal squids as the commonly used lure in the attempt to catch the mighty striped bass. His book gives profiles and cross sections of six different block tin squids, some sporting names for famous fishing locations like the Montauk and the Belmar. For variety the old timers would do different things to enhance the tins such as bend them for a desired action, add a pork rind strip to the rear hook, tie feathers to the tail hook or add a stinger hook to the rear hook to make up for short strikes. Camp also makes mention of the metal squids being between 2½ and 4 ounces and painted in various color combinations.

As we do today, the surfcaster from yesteryear constantly played with options and tried to find "a better way." To help us understand more clearly what a surfcaster of Camp's time did in a particular situation, and so you can see the thought process, here is a short excerpt from his book.

*"Some years ago, while fishing at North Point Beach, that narrow strip of sand separating the Atlantic from Barnegat Bay,* [now Island Beach State Park] *I noticed some stripers feeding on a flooded sand bar. I could see the big fish swirl and occasionally a tail would break the surface.*

*For nearly an hour I tried metal squids of various shapes, but the fish ignored them. I happened to have a sand eel squid that had been painted lemon-yellow with a red head.*

*As a last resort I tried it. The result was three fish in five casts. In an experimental mood, I removed this and tried a regular metal squid with a long pork-rind tail hook. I took two fish on this. Then I tried a white feather lure with red-lead head. This also met with the stripers' approval."*

In the early days of surfcasting tin squids were *the* lure of preference quite possibly because they were the *only* lure available. Though they are still a part of the surfcasters selection base, the role of the metal lure has been reduced today due to the numerous "better" options that are available such as poppers or swimmers, both of which would in all likelihood have been used first off in both examples stated above—if they were available.

Despite its reduced role, however, there are times when the metal can do what no other lure can, so let's look further into metal options.

## THE LORE OF METAL

The metal lures that we grew up using are similar to the metals that came before us, used by our fathers and our father's fathers. I have found stored in my basement tins that my grandfather used to fish the beaches in the mid-1960s, still useful and productive today. On occasion I take one of my grandfather's early sand eel imitation squids and use it just for the sake of the family, its previous generations and for nostalgia. I like to re-visit the family's (or any past surfmen's) lore of catching bass on tins that came long, long before I did. There is something cool about standing there fighting a good fish on a tin that your grandfather used, one probably similar to the one that Heilner used back in the early 1900s, for the same stripers that many generations of surf men have used before us all along the coast.

The attraction of a fish to metal is understandable. The flash that it throws while spinning, fluttering or wobbling through the water is seen as an easy target from the fish's eye. The tin, or any metal lure, is more

*"Grandpa's Tins." My grandfather (we called him "BB" for some reason) died when I was 2. I don't remember much personally, but I see him in old photos and 8mm home movies. My grandmother told me they moved to the shore from upstate New York because he loved the ocean and fishing so much, he wanted to be closer. He and my grandmother and mother would come down and live in the garage he built first, while they worked on the main house. I am sure these tins are some that BB used whenever he could sneak away to do some casting.*

quiet than a rattling swimming plug, the reflection of the sun's rays alone must surely catch the fish's eye.

The metal is a first-class fish producer. What I mean here is that once a metal "arrives on the scene" you can have confidence in its ability to catch. When it moves through the water all the fish in the vicinity will take notice! After all it does imitate one of two things: a wounded bait-fish struggling on the bottom or a baitfish that has become separated from the school and is on the flee in a panic-stricken state.

There are four good reasons that I can come up with to prove why metals are a valuable tool in the old plug caster's arsenal. One excellent advantage is casting distance. It can be thrown an unbelievable distance with a powerful deep-loading rod. Sometimes when fish are breaking out past the bar, the metal may be the one thing that can get you into some action.

A metal lure also covers a considerably larger area of water because it can be cast so far, thus increasing your chances of a fish seeing your offering simply because your range is extended by a hundred feet or more. Besides the distance advantage, a metal lure will cast extremely well into a head wind or a wind right in your face. It is there for you when you really need to get it out into fish-filled froth.

The third thing that adds to the metal's value is water penetration. Metals get out there and then they sink instantly to the bottom, and remember, this is where most of the bigger bass hold and hunt. It should be a golden rule for you to make it a point to get an offering below a school of feeding bluefish or bass and this is where the metal wins out over the popper or swimmer. This can be easily done by casting to the outskirts of the school, letting your metal sink and then slowly jigging the tin by lifting and dropping your rod tip while reeling very slowly and staying in contact the entire time. By doing this you stay in a very high percentage area where your chances for strikes are very high and your chances on bigger fish are greatest. The further your tin travels away from the fish activity the smaller your chances will be due to the diminishing fish concentration. Reel in cast again into the "red zone" and work it fervently.

Metals are good imitations of bait. The various shapes and sizes available make metals a very versatile lure style with many applications. There is always room for tins in my surf bag, they go everywhere with me ready at a moment's whim. I usually match my tins which the predominant baits in my area at the time. As an example, if mullet or peanut bunker you go with a Hopkins Shorty, if sand eels and spearing are prevalent go with long skinny profiles such as Ava's or AOK's T-Hex.

## METAL AT NIGHT

As long as I have been fishing I was always told that metal is for daytime fishing only, and only to be used when bluefish raid our beaches. Well I was misinformed, thank you very much. Whoever you were you were wrong!

The black and dark-color tins or metal have become one of my number one options when fishing in the dark under certain conditions. It is one of the most overlooked night lures.

Think about it, why wouldn't metal work in the dark? The advantages again are distance and penetration. My small circle of fishing buddies have been using metals almost exclusively at night at one of our favorite hard-pulling rips with excellent success. When the water pulls hard one of your key demands is water penetration.

The metal here would qualify as a mid-column runner when you add the speed of current to the speed of the retrieve. The faster the current the faster your lure will ride and the higher up the water column it will go. If you reel too fast it will be on the surface. Yes, even with a bottom-dwelling tin. Cast upcurrent, wait briefly for penetration and then reel slowly with occasional twitches or rod lifts.

Being that we only fish these waters at night means the black or dark colored metals are needed and by Joe they work very well! The more I talk to seasoned surf guys, the more I realize how many know the effectiveness of metals at night. I find it funny, but not surprising, that not many talk about them.

I like to fish the black tins at night with a black or purple teaser out in front. The teaser and tin is a good one-two punch, and the two usu-

*The night tins are effective bass takers especially in hard-pulling current. Here are three that I use commonly, top to bottom; Point Jude Black Knights in Butterfish and Mullet, and the 2-ounce AOK Tackle PB-40 in black.*

ally share the take evenly thus adding value to the teaser. A teaser with metal is always a good choice because the teaser will not impede the flight and distance of the tin like it would a metal-lip or a hard plastic swimmer. The metal flies as though no teaser is there.

There are some good tins with a durable black powder-coat finish on the market now. Point Jude Lures and AOK Tackle both put out good black tins for use at night. Point Jude has the Black Knight Series which includes their Po-Gee, Butterfish, and Mullet tins in black, which weigh between 1½ and 2 ounces. I also like the blue Sea Scallop which I find useful at night because it has enough shine to pick up any available ambient light.

AOK also has the PB-40 (2 oz.) in black which I like a lot when peanut bunker dump through the night rips.

Today there is a wide variety of metals on the market. Point Jude Lures spearheaded the wide varieties of legitimate tins today and they carry a diversified selection of tins along with tin accessories. They offer a wide variety of lures to match almost any bait fish in the surf. Swing by their website (*www.pointjudelures.com*) to see the options they offer.

*When you throw metal at night you have to add the teaser to double your chances. Dark color teasers work well, but try various colors until you find one that works.*

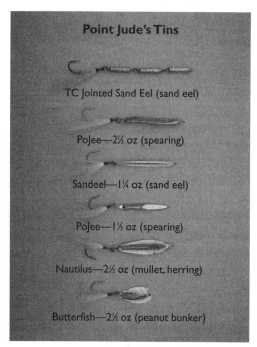

**Point Jude's Tins**

TC Jointed Sand Eel (sand eel)

PoJee—2½ oz (spearing)

Sandeel—1¼ oz (sand eel)

PoJee—1½ oz (spearing)

Nautilus—2½ oz (mullet, herring)

Butterfish—2½ oz (peanut bunker)

*Point Jude Lures has almost everything you need when it comes to tins and metals, as shown in this sampling with the baitfish that each imitates.*

AOK Tackle has some metals out now that are quite impressive and I am gaining more confidence in them all the time. The T-Hex is a very versatile lure that imitates several different baits due to its shape. It has a great side-to-side motion like that of a darter. AOK also carries a unique peanut bunker copy bottom-dweller called the "PB" which is a lock to imitate a wounded juvenile peanut bunker struggling on the bottom.

There are many other tins or metals available from many longstanding manufacturers, names like the Hopkins No=Eql and Shorty, the Acme Kastmaster, Luhr-Jensen's Krocodile, the Crippled Herring and the Ava jigs that are readily found at coastal tackle shops.

## METAL AND SOFT STRUCTURE

One of my favorite ways to catch stripers from the beach is by fishing soft structure on the open beach. The use of a sandbar, a trough and a cut is a super way to catch bass because this kind of structure is where bass hang out. On the open beach where there is no hard structure, such as a jetty or boulders, the bass still feed heavily using the water movement through and over the bottom structure to make it happen for them. When sand eels and other baits such as rainfish, peanut bunker and spearing move through the shallows they swim through mazes of sand, although we don't see it like they do. Bass set up ambush points and use the crashing waves and pulling currents to their advantage. The rough water knocking the baitfish around gives the striper the upper hand. Striped bass use every possible condition in their surroundings to get a meal.

When riding the beach in the fall when the migration is in full swing I look for sandbars in the form of whitewater and waves, shallow water, accompanied with areas of deep water. The deeper water is signified by green, dark water. I look for areas where white meets green, and usually I look for a "crease" that denotes a drastic change in bottom contour and/or colliding currents. The edge of a bar would be a great example. The water will go from a foot deep on the bar to 3 or 4 feet deep in the trough. The drop-off is immediate.

Waves pounding on the bar and water surging across the bar dislodge sand eels or push other types of bait across the shallow bar and then into the deep water of the trough. It is here that the bass are waiting for grub, and this is where your metal comes into play.

When I find a bar with a deep drop-off between me and the bar I go with a metal—which one depends on the bait available, usually something like the T-Hex or Hopkins Shorty. I cast out onto the bar and begin reeling. You will feel a lot of resistance, which is the lure being dragged through the sand. Suddenly you will feel a release, this will be your lure dropping off the bar into the trough and it is here where the hit will occur as bass prowl the trough looking for baitfish that are getting knocked into it. As you feel the tin come free be sure to stay in close

*Sand eel imitations like this AOK T-Hex work just fine when fishing soft structure on the open beach.*

contact as the distinct strike will let you know that there is interest in your offering.

I work an area for a short time, perpetually moving, trying different parts of the bar until I find fish then work the area, take a couple fish and move on to look for the next good spot, working the same pattern I just completed. It works well when the bass are there, but if no fish are found, keep moving along the beach.

Besides the drop-off in the middle of the bar I also like the ends of the bar where the water dumps back into the ocean, the rip or the cut. I call it the corner. Casting to this area is often very productive using the same technique. If the bar and structure are fairly close to the beach where casting distance isn't impacted, I add the teaser which is usually just as productive as the tin. Tins and soft structure work great together.

## MORE ON METAL

Have you ever wondered why there are gold-colored tins available? I have a few but never really used them much so I asked tin man Joe Martins of Point Jude Lures and he said that the gold metals are very good for dirty or murky water, post-storm conditions and for low light conditions. Good to know. He also reminded me that regular metals are good at night under a full moon. The late John Haberek told me of the technique of casting out under a full moon and retrieving very slowly while shaking the rod erratically. He said he won a couple tournaments using that very technique. One night I tried it and it worked, by Joe!

Martins also reminded me that to use metal during blitzes of blues and bass is also very effective not just to cast out and retrieve so as not to get your good wood lure chomped by bluefish, but to use the metal's size and weight to get below the fast moving bluefish down in the water column where the bigger bass hang out. I would have to figure that Haberek's full-moon technique would also in all likelihood work very well in this situation.

One last technique that Joe told me was shared by Tony Chiarappo, a long-time sharpie out on Cape Cod. The Pt. Jude TC Jointed Sand Eel was developed and named after Tony. It obviously imitates a sand eel, and Tony says to cast it and retrieve it slow. If you retrieve it in less than ten minutes, you are reeling too fast. The technique imitates sand eels holding and moving in the sand giving away their location with small puffs of sand. He said that most of the young guys don't have the patience to do it that slow and I would have to say that I probably would fall into that category.

Needless to say there are many techniques and modifications that can be discovered with a little experimentation. The possibilities are endless and if you fish with an open mind, you may surprise yourself.

# 7

# RAKING CALICO CRABS

Striped bass love crabs, all kinds of crabs! One of the most reliable ways to catch striped bass is by baiting up with one of their favorite foods, the calico crab, more commonly known as the lady crab. Calico crabs, sand fleas and other crustaceans are a big-time dinner item for stripers, and they work the best just after the spring migration as the water warms and the bass go into their bottom feeding mode, or what I call the summer feeding pattern.

As summer approaches, bass begin looking down instead of looking up as they did in the spring when they were chasing schools of swimming bait. Fishing with crabs is as reliable as livelining bunker or slinging eels, but it is not a widely-used technique. In fact, it is nearly a lost art. Those surfcasters who do fish with crabs, however, strongly believe in it.

Baiting up with calico crabs begins by raking the surf shallows with a special crab rake to gather a good supply of bait. As you rake, you search for specific crabs that will make the best baits. Anglers who regularly fish

*The calico crab is more commonly known as the Lady Crab because of its good looks. A shallow water, sandy bottom inhabitant, this crab is a favorite food of stripers.*

with crabs set up a tank system to keep crabs until they reach their ideal state—freshly shed. Once they shed they are prime striper baits.

The crab baits need constant care and watching, and you have to make the time commitment to tend to your baits. The entire process of fishing crabs is a high-maintenance chore, but it has a huge upside because one good crab gives you a good shot at catching a good-size fish. New Jersey crabber Lou Rivetti swears to me, "They are the deadliest bass bait out there." Lou would know as he has been fishing with crabs for over 30 years and his biggest crab-caught bass hit the scale at 47 pounds. In this chapter we will look at the techniques surrounding the use of calico crabs in the hunt for striped bass. As you will see this is a technique certainly worth consideration.

## MEET THE CALICO

The calico crab is officially known as the lady crab, *ovalipes ocellatus*; but I have always known it as the calico crab which I am sure was derived from its beautiful spotted shell and magnificent colors. It lives mostly in the shallow sandy water beds of the rolling surf, which is a tough place to hang an address number on because of the wave action and the constantly shifting sands. As the waves roil the dug-in crab, it shifts quickly to reposition itself and then re-buries itself in the sand. The crab lies buried, covered up by sand, waiting for its next meal. It feeds on live or decaying organisms such as fish, crabs and clams, which makes the crab a scavenger and a carnivore. When an unsuspecting fish or worm comes by the crab rockets out of the sand and grabs it with its sharp claws. The claws are not large but they certainly are sharp, two deadly weapons.

For you clam fishermen, in all likelihood it is the calico that you curse when your bait comes back to you in a small ball and all chewed up. You mumble to yourself as you change your bait while somewhere out in the water in front of you sit some very happy calico crabs that just ate at your luncheonette and are waiting for you to serve dessert.

The lady crab is classified as a swimming crab which means it is very mobile and can get up out of the sand and swim as it transports itself from one point to another. Its legs are like flat paddles. Like other swimming crabs such as the blue claw, the lady crab or calico has a relatively thin shell. The calico, therefore, has less protection than other crabs that hide in rocks and which have a harder shell, but it makes up for this liability with speed and camouflage.

The lady crab has an exoskeleton, which means its outer shell supports and protects the body's internal organs, whereas humans for instance have an endoskeleton, the main frame of support is on the inside of the body.

The calico crab can grow up to 4 inches wide though the typical sizes we see most often are between 1 to 3 inches in width. Calico crabs can be found all along the coast from Cape Cod to Texas.

## RAKING CRABS

In order to fish with crabs you first need to gather a supply from the local surf. This is best done in warm weather when the calicos gravitate to the warmer shallow waters. It also needs to be done in calm, clean surf. Waves breaking on you while you are raking will make the task a wet and unfriendly experience, and the constant surges and pushes of water will make it difficult to keep the crabs in the net. Raking is usually done at the bottom three hours of the outgoing and the first three hours of the incoming tide when the shallow beach is most exposed.

The raking is done with a special long-handle rake, made up from a long pole with a rectangular steel frame on the end. It sports 18 long spikes at the bottom and a mesh net or "bag" along the back that will hold the crabs you catch while pulling the rake through the sand. The idea is to scoop the crabs from the sand while letting the sand filter through. Once you begin to rake you must keep the rake moving or else the quick crab will swim out of the net. You will need to figure out a raking pattern that works for you on that day. You want to rake the shallows near the shoreline and don't overlook the sandy areas near jetties, which is also very productive. With some experience you will learn the location of the best areas that hold more calico crabs than others.

To begin raking, set the pole on your shoulder with the spikes facing your feet. Walk backwards dragging the cage through the sand; you want to drag the rake about 10 to 15 feet per swipe. While raking you want to be sure to keep the teeth of the rake point downward as much as possible. If you keep your rake handle too vertical it will cause the spikes to run more horizontal and you will end up impaling crabs. Crab shish kabob, although it may be tasty, is not our intent here!

*The crab extractor; the crab rake is the tool you need for raking the calico from the sandy shallows.*

Once you complete a sweep you then sort the crabs that are in the net. Some fellows wear a glove for handling the crabs but I like the added dexterity of the bare hand. With experience you will learn to quickly examine your raked crabs and be able to tell right away if you have a crab that is serviceable as bait.

When one fishes crabs the main objective is to fish a crab that is soft. A "softy" is also called a shedder. This is your goal as a crab fisherman. Crabs can be fished with hard shells, but the goal of most rakers is to fish them soft or actually post-soft when the new shells are paper thin, about a half hour after the shed—this is what the bass desire most. It is at this time when the crab secretes its enticing oil, and this is the juice that drives bass wild!

A crab that is ready to shed looks darker and the shell looks older. You want "comers," crabs getting ready to shed or the freshly shed softy crabs. "Tin backs" are post-shed crabs that have gotten too hard and can either go back in the water or can be fished in rougher surf because they hold up better. The perfect crab is a crab that has shed within the last half hour and is still soft, but getting firm, not yet a tin back. If you are not sure a crab is ready by looking at it you can check for comers by breaking off the top of the pincer on the claw (not the whole pincher, just the tip). If you find a soft-formed claw, you have found what you are looking for. This crab is getting ready to shed. If you find a mush-like substance the crab could be a long way from becoming a true shedder and is called a "long comer." Throw this one back. If you find an empty claw, this one also is nowhere near ready and it goes back into the wash. If you are lucky and come up with a "shedder" you should not hesitate to fish it right away.

*With handle on the shoulder and a mighty pull, the author works the shallows looking for some prime candidates.*

So that you don't have to walk away from the beach after each sweep to deposit your crabs in a bucket, those crabs you want to keep can be put into a trout creel bag or some other temporary holding container. Softies can be kept in a small plastic bag away from the other crabs in your creel bag. Keep a few zip-type plastic bags in your bag.

It is common to fish with a dead stick while raking, it makes good sense. The raking alone will draw bass into your location as it creates a wonderful chum slick, so not to fish this condition would make one wonder. Getting out of the water quickly when the rod goes down is always a fun adventure, but that is why we fish, to have fun.

While raking you want to get a good amount of crab candidates, maybe 50, and this may take you a couple of hours to do. But, do what you feel is necessary for your needs. Once you have a good number of crab candidates you need to get them home to the tank, and you do this by putting the crabs into a 5-gallon bucket with a few inches of saltwater. An aerator will provide plenty of oxygen during the trip home. A lid on your 5-gallon bucket with a small hole for the aerator hose will keep the crabs happy until you arrive home to your tank.

## THE TANK PROCESS

The tank you set-up at home would usually contain a couple inches of sand and plenty of saltwater. The crabs will bury themselves in the sand and the sand will aid them when they shed. The most serious crab fishermen have their tanks set-up with aerator and filter and all the components similar to what a typical home fish tank would have, only it contains saltwater not fresh. It is here that the crabs are kept and watched until they shed. Then they become optimal bass baits.

There are stages to the crab's shedding cycle and it is important for you to know them. I want to review the stages to make sure the process is clear. It begins with the crab in its normal state with a hard shell. Crabs shed once a month, they leave their old shell by actually crawling out of it, and then a new shell hardens in its place, which will now be roughly one-third bigger than the old shell. At first, the new shell is literally soft, much like soft-shell blue crabs that you buy at the seafood market or restaurant. Once the old shell is shed, the crab stays soft in saltwater for about an hour to an hour and a half before becoming hard again.

Crabs that are getting ready to shed have been nicknamed comers, which means they are about to come out of the shell. They are identified by color. The shell becomes bluish brown and the claws shade towards red. At this stage they will bed in the sand and you, as the watchman, need to monitor the tank to be ready when a crab sheds. Once a crab sheds it is dinner time for all the other crabs around; loyalties and friendships go right out the window. Shedders need to be taken out of the tank immediately. This is done with a dip net. Some crabbers keep a second tank for the shedders exclusively. You will want to leave the crab in saltwater for approximately twenty minutes to a half hour after a shed so that it will firm up. A soft crab on the hook is like mush, it still works, but the ones left for a little while stiffen up and are optimal. The tank should be checked often and around the clock.

Once the crab sheds and the shells firms up a bit, it's now ready to be fished, but we need to get it to the beach at the right time and in the

*This 45-gallon tank has the bottom covered with crushed coral as the perfect set up for crabs to shed. It holds saltwater and is kept clean with a filter and pump. Once a crab sheds it can be transferred to a secondary tank so it won't get eaten by its "buddies." The dip net is used for retrieving crabs.*

*This type of aerator is common with liveliners and crab men. It gives the crabs plenty of oxygen.*

best condition. The crabs are then neatly stacked on damp paper towels, newspaper or seaweed, and they get stacked diagonally not flat. A small plastic tray with a lid works very well. They are then covered by the same damp cover (paper or seaweed) and refrigerated. They must be kept moist until ready for the ride to the beach. You want to have enough crabs to fish the tidal stage or as long as you are able to fish.

If you have some crabs that have been in the refrigerator for a couple days, you can always refresh them by throwing them back in the tank for a short period before fishing them. Their bodies will replenish in the fresh saltwater.

To get your crabs to the beach, you want to put your trays into a cooler with ice or cold packs covered with a lid. Never expose them directly to the thawing ice water.

## CRAB TERMINOLOGY

*Here are some terms commonly used with crabs.*

**Hard shell crab**: a crab in its normal state, hard shell and natural colorings.

**Comer**: a crab getting ready to shed.

**Shedder**: a crab that is shedding its old shell, about to become a softy.

**Soft shell crab, a "softy"**: a crab that has just shed and its body is soft and vulnerable. This is your target bait.

**Tinback**: a crab that has become hard up just after a shed.

## FISHING WITH CRABS

Once you have gone through all the trouble of collecting your crabs and getting them ready to fish you now get to have some fun and finally attempt to catch some bass. Fishing with crabs is an extremely good way to catch bass consistently, and usually you can count on one good crab catching one good fish.

Bass are scavengers and will do whatever it takes to work up a meal. One of their techniques is rooting along the bottom, as they dig into the sandy shallows with their nose and dislodge tasty morsels from the sand. You may have caught a warm-water bass and noticed that its chin and nose area is red—this is the result of rooting for food. They do this for crabs and sand fleas, and they also do it for sand eels.

*The inexpensive trout creel works great as a temporary holding place for crabs until you get back to the beach.*

The scent put out by the shed crab gives the bass a point of focus, and makes finding the crab a lot easier. The scent of a crab is a strong attraction for the bass, and that's why fishing with crabs is such a good technique. This is also why you want to fish while you are raking. The raking is an equivalent to chumming, and as the rake stirs the bottom and sometimes spears crabs, it's leaving a scent trail that calls in bass from near and far.

It is important to know that striped bass are not the only predators that love shedder crabs. Many other shallow-water dwellers feed on them as well and a floating shedder crab is an easy meal for nuisance fish, like sea robins. If sea robins or some other predator are present, pack up and move on.

The crab gets tied onto a baitholder-type hook with elastic thread. As a rule the smaller crabs do not get impaled on the hook. The elastic thread is wrapped around the crab several times front to back then diagonally across the shell a few turns on each side, and the legs are left to hang free. Bigger crabs can be impaled on the hook to help keep the bigger, heavier body offering from flying off, especially during the cast. Be sure, however, that you rig the crab so it looks natural.

Fishing two rods is a good strategy. One can be fished long with the bait cast far out and over the bar, and the other short and inside the bar. You need to find where the fish may be rooting or hunting for a meal. Most fellows use a 9- to 10½-foot rod when fishing crabs. Note that many a rod has been pulled into the surf by a big bass, so be sure that when deadsticking that your sand spikes are well dug in. Big fish don't play around.

On the business end is a fishfinder rig. Tie a barrel swivel at the end
of the main fishing line and then add a 24-inch length of mono leader
with another barrel swivel at its terminal end. The fishfinder is slid onto
the leader before tying the second barrel swivel in place, and with small
stopper beads on either side of it. Rivetti makes up pre-tied leaders about
14 to 20 inches long. To one end he ties on a baitholder hook, to the
other a Duolock snap. The hook size can be anywhere from 4/0 up to
8/0, depending on size of the crab baits and size of the bass you expect
to catch. He carries pre-tied leaders in a plastic bag in his pocket, and
while fishing one crab he pre-rigs a second crab and keeps it on ice. This
way there is no time wasted in the tying process. He simply opens the
snap, takes the used hook off and puts the new one on with a fresh bait.

Crabs are best fished when the surf has some gently rolling lift and the
waves are forming just beyond the wash. Rough water is not the preferred
condition but can be fished with tin backs. Where the crab is placed in the
waves is important. When deciding on where to cast your crab, you want
to find the place where the second or third wave lifts or begins to form,
this is a good starting point. This will lift the semi-buoyant crab as each
swell passes, drawing the bass in to investigate the tumbling crab.

*The Eagle Claw bait holder is the go-to hook. Some believe that the leftover elastic thread
holds crab scent.*

An important point to realize is that a live shedder cannot dig into the sand and is very buoyant, making it even more of a target for hungry bass. Lob cast your crab into the lift of the wave. Note that I said lob; casting hard will in all likelihood make a mess of your crab and all the hard work you just put yourself through will be wasted.

While some anglers prefer heavy sinkers I have always believed that you only need enough weight to hold your bait on the bottom and to hold fast. In calm surf with no big heave or hard-pulling current, 4 to 6 ounces will do.

When crabbing you will need to develop your own series of systems that you can work with and be comfortable with. There is no wrong way or right way, only a productive way, a way that works well for you. What I have listed above is a guideline for fishing a reliable and fascinating way of catching bass. Like everything else figure out your system and let it work for you.

*Bob Bottino (right) was a trendsetter when it came to raking and fishing crabs. A lot of the techniques that he developed are still used by some of today's best crabbers. Bottino was also a very good liveliner. He is pictured here in 1980 with another great surfcaster, Bobby Matthews, in Asbury Park, New Jersey, the two sporting a pair of 30 pounders.*

In closing and since I am from New Jersey, I would be remiss if I did not write something on raking calico crabs without mentioning the name Bob Bottino. He was a die-hard bass man and a trendsetter when it came to raking, keeping and fishing crabs. Many of the really good New Jersey crab fishermen were taught by Bob and have followed his techniques. They saw him as the one of the best and one of the most knowledgeable crabbers of our era. Bottino took bass of over 50 pounds while fishing with crabs. He'll be missed by many.

# 8

# CLAMS FOR BAIT

I strongly believe that if you want to learn how to catch striped bass regularly, then you should learn how to fish with clams and become proficient at doing so. At times clam fishing will far out-produce any other bait offering, and at times will be the only way to catch fish. The trick is to throw the clam at the right place and at the right time. Perhaps clamming is not the most romantic way to catch bass, but it certainly is productive.

Clamming is a good strategy for those starting out because it lays good groundwork for a beginning striper man and develops many of the basic techniques that are needed to become skilled in the surf. Skills such as presentation, careful casting, reading the water, fighting fish and washing up fish at the end game can be all honed. Now I am not saying that clam fishing is just for novice fishermen, for that certainly is not true. A good striper man needs balance and needs to know all the approaches and options for catching stripers.

Usually after a big blow, such as a northeaster or hurricane, the "mighty" clam can be terribly effective. During the high surf and pounding waves caused by those storms, clams get uprooted from the bottom and tossed from their beds. They are then crushed by the force of the waves then washed onto the beach where the juice of crushed dying clams draws stripers of all sizes and shapes (hopefully fat). I have foolishly stood in the pounding surf and have felt the power of waves move the ground under my feet and the force of waves actually moved me back a foot or two, now that is powerful stuff (yes I got the hell out of the water quickly). The clam crush makes its own chum slick and bass will come from far and near to dine on an easy meal. It is a time when the surfcaster can really cash in on some bass.

Another good time to use clams is in the summer months when the water is calm and quiet. Bass at this time swim very close to the beach in low-light conditions feeding on crabs, sand fleas or mole crabs. They are in their "look down" mode nosing and rooting in the sand. A clam presentation at this time is easy pickings for them and right in their strike zone.

*Offering a bass a fresh bait is the closest thing to a sure bet as you can get. Using fresh, (live) clams are proven producers especially when tossed into the angry surf.*

Clams are good anytime throughout the season because they are a natural bait that is always present and never goes "out of season." Remember, clams don't migrate, they move too slowly, so they are always a good bait.

## CHOOSING THE BAIT

When fishing clams I have a fairly strict rule on what kind of clam I'm looking for and I can sum it up in one word—fresh! This is very important. Clams that are still alive inside the shell are the best kind of clam. I jokingly call this live-lining since they are still moving when I put them on the hook.

When choosing your clams from a bushel bag or tackle shop cooler, look for clams that are closed and heavy. If they are heavy it means they are still holding water and thus they are still alive. You can also whiff the clam, if it smells pretty bad, let it go.

The only other clam bait that I would consider if I had to choose an alternative to fresh would be salted clams. Salted clams are fresh clams that have been shucked and placed in a sea-salt mixture and then refrigerated. These clams become tough and I jokingly call them shoe leathers. They have tremendous holding power on the hook, and that can also play to your advantage when you feel that long casts are important. With a salted clam you can load your rod and really catapult your clam out there. I also feel that salted clams cull out smaller bass and junk fish, and they are so tough that crabs do not destroy the bait as fast. Small bass cannot ingest the large foot as they would with a fresh clam. So when there is a lot of competition for your clam bait besides that of the striper, a salted clam may be a good consideration. A decent-sized salted clam foot will stay on the hook longer because of its toughness thus it will remain in the strike zone longer where a patrolling bass can get a good look or a good sniff.

Frozen clams should never be considered as they become mush when thawed and have close to zero holding power when cast out.

## SHUCKIN' CLAMS

If you are going to fish fresh clams you need to know how to shuck one. It is fairly quick although a little messy so it is a good idea to keep a towel handy for clean up. If you plan on a long weekend of fishing, or want to lay up a supply of salted clams, consider buying a bushel of clams for you or a few friends together. Find a clam distributor and you will see a huge savings.

It's important that you use a clam knife, which just about every tackle shop sells, and not a regular knife. The clam knife is short and has a rounded point and is not very sharp. I don't think it can cut you but it is sharp enough to cut the clam.

Grab the clam and lay it flat in the palm of your hand, if you are right-handed you will want to hold it in your left hand. Near the back of the clam there are two big muscles that the clam uses to open and close the shell. Cut these two quarter-sized muscles with your clam knife. You do not want to cut into the clam too deep and hit the foot of the clam, that big meaty tongue in the middle, because you want to use that on your hook.

Cut these muscles by sliding the knife into the clam just in front of the muscles and cut towards the back; remember stick your knife in just far enough to sever the muscle. Cut both sides of the muscle and the clam will open easily.

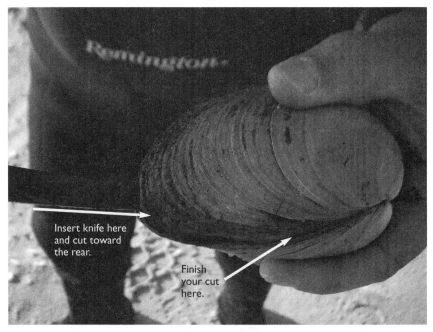

*All clams have this slit that accepts the knife perfectly. Insert your clam knife there and cut towards the back, severing the muscle that keeps the clam closed.*

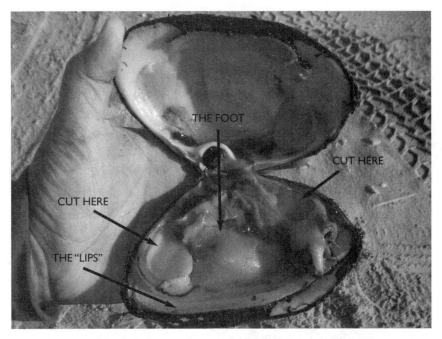

*Once open you will have two separate baits available; the foot and the "lips." Do one more cut clockwise from the rear all the way along the perimeter and all of the clam's innards will be free. Keep the knife right on the bottom of the shell as to not cut the foot.*

Run the knife along the perimeter of the rest of the clam, both shells. By doing this you will cut what I call the lips from the shell. You should have all the pieces now in one shell. Toss the half empty shell into the water for chum.

Now that the shell is open, you will have the innards in a tidy little package and you will have two specific baits, the foot and the lips. They will both serve as clam baits, but on different hooks.

The foot of the clam goes on the big 6/0 hook. I hook the clam foot once through the tip of the foot and then turn the hook and drive it deep into the center rear of the clam, but not too far back where the flesh gets very soft. I push the clam way up the shaft of the hook past the baitholder and even past the eye sometimes. When tying a clam on with elastic thread, it is at this point you want to wrap the entire piece thoroughly.

The two leftover lips go on the top hook, the 4/0. Running through this lip section is a very tough area of flesh, and you want to get your

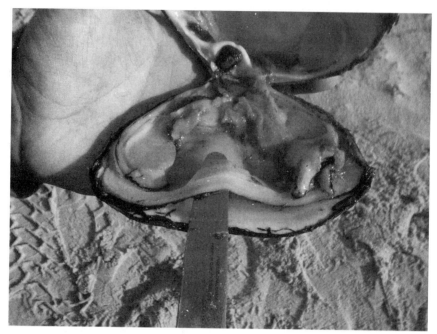

*The last cut around the perimeter frees the lips and the rest of the clam. Do not cut the foot.*

hook through this tough muscle. Once you do, the lip will stay on the hook for a long time. You can check it by jerking on the lip, if you got it hooked right it will stay on. If you missed you will be holding it in your hand. Try again!

## THE MULLER CLAM RIG

I have used this rig for many years and it has taken a good number of bass for me. It was originally shown to me by a good fellow named Ed Brusso many years ago, a man who taught me my way around clams. I have never seen this rig anywhere else and Ed is no longer with us, so to avoid confusion I call it the Muller Rig.

I start off with a 20-inch length of 40-pound test mono. About a third of the way down from the top I tie a dropper loop. On one end I tie either a loop or tie on a barrel swivel, this will connect to my running line, the other end gets a good size, quality three-way swivel. The dropper loop gets a 4/0 gold baitholder hook which is attached by a short leader of mono. Off the three-way would be a 10-inch dropper leader to a 6/0 gold baitholder hook. Off the third eye of the three-way swivel would be a large Duolock snap that would hold the sinker.

I use the lightest sinker weight possible—just enough weight to hold bottom. I usually start with a 3-ounce sinker under typical flat conditions, and I always use a bank sinker for clamming with this particular rig. The theory behind it is that the fish picks up the bait and starts moving away. The sinker in turn slides along slowly causing some resistance. When the fish realizes some-

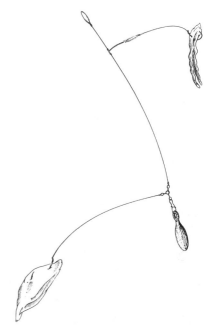

*The Muller Rig*

thing is wrong it will quickly accelerate away from the situation thereby hooking itself while doing so. In this case, I want the fish to feel the resistance, not like when using a fish-finder rig. This rig works like a charm.

I always use baitholder hooks with the small barbs along the shank. They really work wonders for holding onto bait, thus the name baitholder hooks.

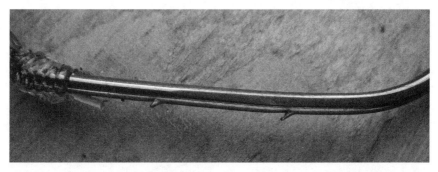

*The Eagle Claw baitholder hooks have barbs along the shank. Though small these are important in helping keep your bait up on the shank.*

If circle hooks are your preference, this rig is ideal since there is no hook setting involved, the fish hooks itself. The circle hook is made to lip hook the fish, or hook it in the corner of the jaw, and it does so almost every time a fish is caught.

Is this rig the one and only? Is it the miracle rig that can catch when everything else can't? No! There are other rigs and even a single hook off a three-way or a fishfinder rig will work well too. This rig, however, works very well and it's here if you need it. You may search and find another one that gives you confidence and you will do fine.

## TACKLE & EQUIPMENT CHOICES

Clams catch a lot of fish, but clams as a rule don't usually take huge bass consistently. They do at times take trophy bass, just not very often. So don't kill yourself with a massive rod and reel combo. I like to clam with a 9-foot rod and a matching reel. I do not spend a great deal of money on my bait rods and reels, especially my clamming equipment because they do not have to take the abuse that the plugging combos do. They are not held in our hands for long periods of time, and the reels are not put through the rigors of constant casting and retrieving over and over as plugging reels are. After the cast, the rod and reel is placed in a sand spike and it rests there until a fish takes the bait.

Besides the rod and reel you will need: long sand spikes, clam knife, extra rigs, sinkers and hooks, pliers, a rag or towel, a light, perhaps bug spray and a bucket to carry everything in—at least this is the way I do it. It is not a bad idea to keep a tin, a shad, a popper and a swimming plug in the bucket just in case a school of blues or bass comes cruising past while you are bait fishing.

## LET'S GO FISHING

When fishing fresh clams you need to handle them with care for they are not the hardiest of meats. Once you have everything baited up it is now time to cast away. I like to find deep water with good current or water movement when choosing a spot to fish. There is usually plenty of water movement along the beach anyway so the scent of the clam baits will be carried by the current and calling in fish from afar. For some reason unknown to me, many guys feel like they have to hug a jetty monopoliz-

*When baiting the hook try to get the hook through the foot twice and through the tougher tip area. Back towards the belly (the lighter area) the meat gets very soft and tears easily. When you retrieve to check your bait, you can turn the hook back into the bait again (the third time) for added holding power on your second cast.*

ing the pocket. Little do they know that the open beach's current flow will carry the scent a lot further than the swirling water of the jetty pocket. By fishing right next to a jetty you are in a spot with less water flow, which limits half of your potential to carry scent to fish quite a distance down the beach.

When casting out you do not want to load the rod trying to blast your bait into orbit, this is not necessary and in all likelihood will cost you clam baits as they fly off the hook and hit the lady shell hunting along the shoreline. I like to find the deepest water in the trough or cut and then lay the bait right in the middle of that area or just off that area in the slowing water or eddy. Just lob or toss your cast gently into the wash keeping your bait intact. I usually like to get my bait into 3 to 5 feet of water or more and most troughs would fall into this category. Remember bass are in no way afraid of shallow water.

I like to check my bait every ten minutes or so based on the fact that everything under the surface, especially pesky bait stealers and crabs, likes to eat clams.

As a rule you don't want to fish mid-day. Dusk to dawn is the best time when bass cruise the beach. Fishing from morning darkness until sun up is probably the most productive and most realistic time for the average working man. You can hit your fish and get to work with a smile on your face.

## TOO MUCH CLAMMING?

I believe that fishing clams for stripers is a technique that you need in your arsenal of strategy options, a weapon to be brought at certain times under specific conditions. I like to fish clams when the surf is riled and angry and the stripers are at close range on a gut-stuffing party. I also don't mind an occasional lazy Sunday afternoon on the beach relaxing and soaking clams listening to the radio or some music, and just simply enjoying the day.

Some surf fishermen, however, have come to believe that clam fishing is the one and only way to catch stripers. There is nothing wrong with focusing on a sole technique and mastering it, however, I see more and more fishermen that only clam fish. They know no other way!

One overcast October afternoon the bass and blues were going crazy along Island Beach State Park. The usual fleet of buggies were chasing the birds and fish down the beach, the blitz was widespread and there was plenty of action for everyone, but you had to keep moving to stay in front of the schools. I watched in utter amazement as the fish rambled through and the clam fishermen, of which there were many, sat nervously by their bait rods waiting for a hit and watching the guys throwing plugs score on cast after cast. The clam guys were also getting angry at the artificial guys and words were sometimes exchanged. They were getting frustrated that everyone throwing poppers or swimmers was hooking up while their bait rods stood lifeless.

At one point as I lingered, looking down the beach and watching the spectacle when plugger meets baiter (I find a little bit of humor in it in some odd way), I couldn't help but notice a clammer that ran down to his rod, grabbed it from the spike and began reeling in quickly. "At last!" I thought, "There's one that has seen the light and he is switching over to a popper or something!" Boy was I surprised when he ran back down to the surf after a few moments with a fresh clam on the hook which he proceeded to heave into the melee. I scratched my head and I was utterly flabbergasted. Needless to say he went fishless.

*Know when to say when. Fishing conditions change, so change with them. There comes a time when artificials dominate the scene. Stay flexible and your days in the surf will be memorable. Dave Arnold sports a small bass that fell for a Gary2 swimmer.*

This situation cemented in my head the danger of being absorbed with the "mindset of a clammer," a scary predicament where you get stuck in a single dimension. They cannot change their ways, and cannot be flexible enough to adjust to a changing situation or condition. I always assumed that you fish to catch fish, and if the fish that you are trying to catch are in front of you and all you need to do is make a small change or two to catch a few, why wouldn't you do that?

Now I am certainly not talking about all clam fishermen here, but I have noticed a frightfully large number that see bass fishing through the "clam" funnel. As a bass man you will enjoy the fishing a lot more when you stretch yourself to learn and do many of the strategies that this book mentions. Not only will it give you wider range in your ability to catch in different situations, but it will also supply you with plenty of challenges and interesting areas of growth. Learning is gratifying and fun.

# 9

# CHUNKING BAIT

There are several techniques that are reliable for consistently taking big striped bass; live lining, snagging and dropping, eeling and chunking. If a big fish is in your dreams, plans and expectations, don't limit yourself by being unprepared to offer up an acceptable bait when a cow moves into your proverbial pasture.

Preparation and patience are the keys to successful chunking. The gathering of fresh bait and then waiting for the cow to come along to your bait is in a nutshell what chunking is all about. Sounds simple, but there's plenty of hard work and preparation required. Fresh chunks of bait fish such as mackerel, squid or menhaden, will put you a lot closer to realizing that big-bass dream than will an artificial lure.

Is chunking a technique that you will use all season long? No, not really. You chunk when the time is right. You strike while the iron is hot. You want to put yourself in the correct place at the right time with the right offering. But, there are times during the season when the chunk will be your only path to a big bass.

As I sought out trophy-size bass, truly big fish, I mean mid–30 pound class and up, I realized two things. One is that the fish has a path or a route upon which it is traveling. Two, I have a route upon which I am traveling. What I want to do is to make those two different paths, the one that the fish is on and mine, collide. You make this connection happen by knowing where the big fish are located, when they are traveling in your area and by knowing what they are feeding on. It's essential that you present the fish an enticing offering that you *know* the fish will take. When these two paths cross you will then have the opportunity that every surfcaster dreams of—Lunkerville!

Another key factor is to play the percentages, the longer you have your presentation out there in the great fish's path, the better your chances are of having a hungry fish take your bait. This is not directly tied to chunking, but if you go down to the train station and the train isn't there, you have to wait for it. Whether you know the train schedule or not, you know sooner or later the train has to come down the tracks. My point here is that chunking leaves an acceptable bait in the path of a cow so that when the big fish does finally travel by, you will be there waiting. Chunking is the only technique where you can leave an offering in a "big fish zone" for a prolonged time period.

*Chunking is a one-way ticket to big fish. Here's a 51 pounder I took on a bunker head one June evening. Good bait and patience will get you your big fish.*

# A MYSTERY

One of the great mysteries to me about the surf contingent is why more guys do not fish with chunk baits. I hear things like, "It's boring." Or, "It's dumb." Some say, "It's only for the white-bucket brigade." Others think it's a lazy man's fishery. "Aw, I couldn't do that; sit on a chair for a couple hours," but I bet that if I could promise you that by hanging around for a couple of hours the biggest bass you ever caught would come by and give you a shot at catching it, that you would not think chunking is so boring. Would you?

Do you think those who came before us, the men of myth and legend, those who caught bass by bait fishing had an outlook like, "Aw, this is boring but I'll fish anyway?" For many years man has used chunks of fresh bait to take big bass. Chunking is by far the oldest method used to catch striped bass from the surf. It is well documented that the Cuttyhunk Club, formed in 1864, chunked bass (with lobsters by the way!) for over 40 years until 1911 when it finally closed the doors. There were other clubs such as the Pasque Island Fishing Club and of course the early pioneer chunk fishermen of Newport, Rhode Island.

Today techniques are similar, but life is more complex. Some of the best bass men use chunking as one of the most important big guns in their big-bass arsenal of techniques. Do they chunk all the time? All season long? No. It is a specific tactic used when big bass and big baits become available in the area where they fish. It is done at the right time and in a strategic spot. Remember that I am referring to big bass here, 30 pounds and up. The monster bass capabilities of the chunking strategy pulls it out of the minor leagues of surfcasting and puts it right to the top spot. If I didn't think that it gave me a really good shot to catch a really big bass, I wouldn't do it. The fact that it can take fish that no other technique can is enough for me to want to learn it and utilize it as valuable strategy.

I know that a lot of surfcasters out there believe that chunking is a lazy way to fish and that fish caught with this technique are somehow not "legitimate" catches, but really the bottom line is that if you want trophy bass, you have to do whatever it takes to get one. If you want to be an artificial purist, well, fine, but I want to catch big bass despite what the cynics say.

To take it one step further, if you and I chose a month that big fish come around the area, and you fished artificials, and I fished chunks, do you think you could out fish me when it came to size? I very respectfully doubt it. I believe in chunking for large fish that much.

*The trick is fresh bait. If the bait isn't fresh, don't waste your time. There are always good Seinfeld reruns on the TV.*

## THE ART OF CHUNKING

Chunking for stripers gives you an incredible chance at hitting a home run, when it is done correctly. The trick is not really a secret, but it is often overlooked or ignored by those who use bait for bass in hopes of a true lunker. I have come across some fishermen who have said they have tried chunking, but had no luck. The problem could have been the freshness of the bait selection. Whatever the bait you decide to use, squid, bunker, mackerel or shad, make sure it is prime and as fresh as it can possibly be.

When thinking about the work involved in gathering my bait prior to fishing with bunker chunks, I often wonder if it's worth all the effort, but once a big bass lies at my feet the answer is, "Hell yeah! It's worth it." I remember the evening I hit a 38 pounder just before dark. As I finally washed the bass onto the beach I let out a yell, something like "Yeah!" I was pumped. Some yuppie dog-walker comes up to me and says "Wow, you must be really happy!" I yelled, "Hell, yeah!" at him. The guy probably thought I was a jerk for yelling at him, but I was just happy with the fish, of course, and even more relieved that the hard work leading up to the fish had just paid a dividend. You know we gamble when we fish.

The work in chunking comes in gathering and keeping fresh bait. While talking to a friend of mine on Cuttyhunk he said that one of his favorite ways to catch big stripers in the spring is by jigging some fresh squid from the fish docks at the harbor and then chunking them at Churches Beach a short distance from there. This tactic, as simple as it was, seems like a no-brainer. It is no secret that Vineyard casters have been quietly using squid for years. While most want to clean the squid and prepare a delicious meal, some good surfcasters see the value of fresh bait. My point is that it's not what's on the menu; it's the freshness of the meal that counts.

I have been victimized by poor bait, and to illustrate how important it is, let me tell a story about an experience I had while chunking one time with what was supposedly "fresh" bunker one night. I sat idle all night, no bass, not even a sniff, while friends of mine just a couple hundred yards away pounded big fish into oblivion all night while I went hitless. After doing some investigating, I came to find that my bait was not as fresh as I thought, having bought it at a local tackle shop. My bait was okay for crabbing in the river, but not for serious chunking. I paid the price. Success with big fish on fresh bait does not come from your simply hooking a piece of bait onto your hook and casting it into the sea and then waiting for a titan to swim into your zone and eat your offering, but rather the upper hand will come through the hard work you invest to collect your fresh bait and keeping it fresh until the time comes for you to use it.

I would like to hammer the fresh bait nail home one last time (as if I haven't done it enough up to this point) by saying that I was chunking a Long Island beach with my buddy "Crazy" Alberto Knie and a couple other good fellows a few years back. We had chunked for large bass all night and nothing of note was caught through the night watch. We kept fishing through false dawn as the tidal stage became optimal. The bunker we were using for bait was becoming questionable, and as you can now guess, I am extremely fussy about the freshness of my bait. The bunker had sat in the cooler all night, iced and cold, but I was losing confidence in it as it began getting soft and bloody.

*The skate bass. I used the freshest bait I could get my hands on and the payoff was a 25 pounder at dawn.*

Alberto is a funny guy and he likes to eat all kinds of fish—folktales precede him. Anyway we hit some good sized skates throughout the night, some pushing between 8 to 10 pounds. If the skate was of decent sizes Al would take the wings for the dinner table. Well as I was standing there tending my rod I glanced down to see a wingless skate lying near me, looking up at me. I began to think; "That is some fresh meat right there. It was recently killed and must have some good meat on it somewhere, I wonder if it would interest a bass. It should!" I threw out my idea to the boys with no serious takers so I spiked my rod and went looking for the knife. I went over to the skate and cut off a big chunk about an inch thick and 5 inches long. I reeled in my bunker and changed baits. The guys kind of snickered, and I did too, but I figured it was the freshest meal in town. I need to stand by my beliefs! I cast it out and within 15 minutes I had a 25-pound bass on the beach. We all laughed—mostly in disbelief.

The motto of the story is two-fold; one is to use fresh bait. Two is to keep an open mind.

## GETTING A HEAD

Chunking is best when you fish strictly with the heads of the baitfish. A bunker head usually produces the bigger fish. Fishing heads automatically culls out smaller fish as smaller fish can't take an entire head like a big fish can, it just won't fit in their mouth. Heads are also bluefish proof 95 percent of the time. Blues don't like bunker heads, and even during a feeding rampage they will eat the fleshy body and then let the head sink to the bottom, much to the contentment of the big bass waiting below.

The head is also rich in protein and "juice." I am not sure exactly what the juice is, maybe cerebral fluid, but whatever it is the bass love it. I think a bunker head is a fun snack for a big bass probably the equivalent of a Dunkin Munchkin for a human.

## GATHERING THE BAIT

Gathering your bait can be done in several ways; buy it from a bunker boat, tackle shop or fish market, or catch it yourself. The first three methods require cash, the last requires skill with a cast net, or you can snag the bunker. If you can find bunker close to shore you can often snag a cooler full in a very short time.

Once you have your fresh bait, you need to keep it very fresh by icing it. To preserve the natural slimy coating I like to put the baits in plastic bags. The fresh bait has to be firm not mushy, it has to have natural coloring, the eyes cannot be red, the fish cannot be stressed or physically mangled and it cannot smell funky.

The bait will be in good shape if it was chilled since being caught and if it had no exposure to warm air or sunlight. It absolutely cannot have been pre-frozen before you bought it or it will be reduced to soft mush when it is thawed again and will not be a worthy bait.

My personal rule is that the bait I use has to be caught the same day. I used to just buy some bunker out of local shop's coolers, labeled "fresh bunker," until I found out that sometimes the fresh bunker was caught very early on the same morning, but it was then trucked for four hours in the hot sun with no ice before it hit the shop's ice-filled coolers. This was not good!

A friend of mine has the ideal system to gather bait. He goes out in his boat, snags or nets bunker, and keeps them in his livewell until he gets back to the dock. He then uses these fresh, chilled baits to chunk for striped bass in the surf that same night. This is the best possible scenario.

*You can't fish with bunker for big bass without using a head. Bunker heads cull small fish, big bass can't refuse them when presented correctly. Here Anna wrestles with a lunker.*

Since I don't have a boat I try to track the local bunker boat when it is sailing. I try to meet the boat at the dock and get the bait from the crew. This is an unreliable and difficult task, however, since the boat has no set hours. Still I need to go to great lengths to find my fresh bait.

## KEEPING FRESH BAITS

Whether you snag, cast net it, or buy it from a bait boat or a tackle shop, once you have a fresh load of bait, it is vitally important for you to keep it in perfect shape until ready for use.

I carefully pack my bait on ice, however, the ice must not come in direct contact with the fish's "skin" or body and the bait must never sit in water, fresh or salt. The slime on the bait is very important to success. Crushed ice is best but if not available, regular cubed ice is the second best choice.

One way to keep baits cold and fresh is to first lay down a layer of ice in the bottom of the cooler and then lay out a row of fresh baits. Place the baits in plastic bags, like the kind you get at a supermarket, and tie the open end closed. You can pack three to five bunker per bag. After you have a layer of bunker in the cooler, add another layer of ice, then more bagged bunker. Keep this up until the cooler is full. The plastic bags keep the melting ice from washing the slime off the baits, and your bunker will be in perfect shape.

For a night session of chunking I usually like to have at least 30 baits on hand. My rule of thumb is one bait per rod every fifteen minutes. I usually fish two rods which equals eight baits an hour, multiplied by how many hours I will fish. For example if I am going to fish four hours with two rods, I will need 32 baits (I usually use just the heads). If bait is hard to come by I will use chunks (other parts of the body) or perhaps I will go down to just one rod.

## IDEAL FISHING

The best time of the year to chunk will vary along the coast. New Jersey gets its bunker a little earlier than Rhode Island or Massachusetts, depending on where you live and fish, so you have to be alert and check with your buddies, tackle shops and other sources that may have solid, reliable reports. For example when adult bunker are in the area and in close proximity to the beach, I spend a lot of time tracking fish, watching the water for bunker schools or watching boat activity, listening to reports, visiting shops, talking to friends or other fishermen, whatever it takes.

Once I have an area identified I then want good surf conditions, and in my experience big bass like calm, clean water and darkness, at which time they cruise the beach looking for easy pickings. Rough water does not work for the chunker, at least this chunker. Tide does not play a big part in my decision-making as much as wind direction. A wind from over my shoulder will give me optimal surf conditions with flat water. I also want water moving along the shore to carry the sweet bunker smell to nearby striped bass.

I usually fish long sessions of three to six hours, biding my time and waiting for my "guests" to arrive. Please realize that chunking does take a tremendous time commitment, but the more you do it the better your chances of hooking up. I have gone for three weeks without a bass at times, and then again had periods of fish every night for a week straight. One thing I do not want to do here is discourage a person that can only fish once or twice a week. If you do it, be patient and stay vigilant, the fish will come. Don't let a fishless night or couple of nights discourage you. You must be mentally tough.

*The beach equipment for chunking. Chunking calls for long hours which may require a chair to rest weary legs. The long aluminum sand spikes have to be strong enough to hold the weight of an angry giant—leave the PVC at home. The cooler keeps the bait cool and crisp until it goes on the hook and the bucket carries all the necessities.*

## SLECTING THE RIGHT TACKLE

Chunking calls in big fish, and big fish require big equipment. This is not a place to fool around with wimpy tackle. Consideration of a lot of variables, such as terrain and structure, surf conditions and the size potential of the fish go into deciding which rod you choose for chunking, but I can safely say that a rod between 10 and 12 feet rated for 6 ounces or more will do the job for you under most conditions.

The reel has to be something that you feel comfortable in using. Conventional tackle is a traditional chunker's reel, but I would be wrong to tell you that it's the only reel-option. I have caught a lot of really big fish on spinning reels. Whichever you choose, spin or conventional, the reel needs to have a generous line capacity and a very good drag system.

Sand spikes are very important when it comes to chunking. I'm not going to get into the age old argument over spiking your rod (leaving it sit in the sand spike) versus holding your rod, but I will say that there are times when you should leave the rod in the sand spike while you are soaking your bait. If and when a big fish takes the bait and heads off the beach at 20 knots, you have to make sure your spikes will hold the rod and not get pulled down and into the water. I use 5-foot aluminum sand spikes and when properly spiked they will hold any fish that we can catch.

Your terminal tackle must always be fresh (new everything) when you chunk because there's no room for compromise. I recall a conversation with big bass specialist "Iron" Mike Everin a few years back where he emphasized over and over to me that you need to re-tie and change hooks and use fresh line when you fish for large striped bass. I agree with him fully, and this attention to detail has to be heightened when big fish are on order. Mike knows the pull of a big fish, and he has taken many a cow. He knows what it takes, so I listen intently when he speaks.

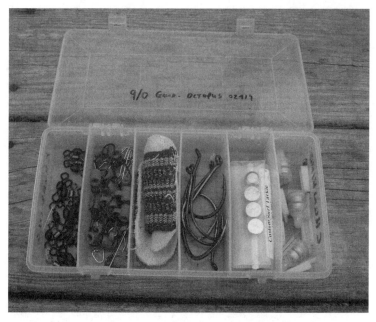

*My chunking tray organizes and carries all of my small important tackle when on the beach. Beside the obvious tackle, I have Red-Eye lights which let me see my rod tips in the night. Finger sheaths for when casting heavy weight. With a spinning set-up, I tighten my drag down all the way and put the finger sheath on—when fishing braid a small slip in the drag while casting will cut a bare finger.*

When I'm chunking, I always use fresh line on the reel, new top-quality swivels, top-shelf hooks and fresh heavy mono leader material. I leave no stone unturned and no room for error. All knots are checked and tested, and new leaders tied on throughout the session.

When chunking under typical open-beach conditions, I like 50-pound Sufix Performance Braid, SPRO barrel swivels, 100-pound test Triple Fish (or equal) monofilament leader material and Gamakatsu Octopus-style hooks in either 9/0 or 10/0. I use fishfinders that are braid friendly such as those made by Long Range. If you use the standard fishfinder your braid will cut right through the soft plastic.

I carry a small Plano tray in my surf bucket to hold all my small tackle and necessities, including extra hooks and swivels, fishfinders, Red Eyes (my night lights), and several finger sheaths to avoid line cuts while casting the heavy baits and sinkers. A sharp knife with a serrated blade, a small wood cutting board, several sinkers of 6 or more ounces, a small rag, bug repellant, a light, a spool of leader material and some spare lures (you never know) also go in the bucket.

The rig I use is a simple fishfinder set up. I keep my 100-pound test leader fairly short at no more than 6 to 8 inches. At times a shock leader at the end of the main fishing line will be required and I go with about 16 to 20 feet of 60-pound monofilament tied off to the braid using the Alberto Knot.

# 10

# THE MAGIC OF LIVELINING

Livelining is the act of using a live bait to catch a striped bass, and any seasoned bass man would not argue about how good this special technique really is. It's known for taking bigger fish because the live bait, especially larger live bait, automatically culls out smaller fish. It has to be a pretty big bass to take a live whole mackerel or menhaden. Livelining takes commitment, and it's a technique that requires large quantities of time, effort and patience.

A live bait properly presented to a big fish has a high probability for success, but livelining's work and commitment leave few anglers willing to do the deed. The entire process of gathering bait, preserving the bait and then fishing the bait is tedious, yet that overwhelming joy of watching a large striper come up and inhale your offering will send adrenaline through your veins like nothing else. It is a reward that makes the entire process worth it. The reward of large bass is also a strong motivator when balancing the scales between effort expended verses reward received. In summation, the amount of hard work that goes into the bait collecting and maintenance has a large pay off on the backside and that is why it is a preferred strategy by sharpies along the coast.

Striped bass eat just about anything that swims so if you give them a good offering they will probably eat it wholeheartedly. If you can get a hook into it, it will work as a bass bait: mackerel, menhaden (pogies to New Englanders, bunker to Mid Atlantic fishermen), herring (river and sea), scup (porgies), bergalls, mullet, eels, shad and bluefish—you name it, they eat it.

## PASSION OR OBSESSION?

I would like to share with you a story that will help you to understand what goes into livelining, and though this is a story of a man from yesteryear it still typifies the passion that surfcasters have in their quest for a trophy. It's about a New Jersey surfcaster who fished in a time when big stripers inhabited Jersey waters in the summer months, something that you don't see as often today. It's a story about one man and his quest for big bass and all that goes with it.

Spring is a time surfcasters anxiously look forward to. The warming air and water temperatures bring the herring into the rivers to spawn, and close on their tails are the mighty striped bass. It is not long after that the menhaden, known locally as bunker, enter the river as well. Both are vital forage that striped bass depend on. There is only one thing that bass love more than herring and that is bunker. Tony Saunders from Toms River, New Jersey knew this and he had made the pursuit of herring and bunker as the means of catching big bass his life's passion. In the glory days of big stripers on New Jersey beaches, there was a contingency of men who pursued both the striper and the bait needed to take the fish with extreme vigor. It was common to gather live herring or bunker for bait, and then take them to a jetty in Monmouth County, to fish them in hopes of a trophy. The process was rigorous and time consuming, and there were many who gave up everything, forsaking family and friends, to catch stripers on live bait.

The glory days to which I'm referring ran through the 1980s. Bunker and herring were in plentiful supply and good-size bass ruled the rivers and jetty tips. Saunders was there for the best of these times and he told me the story of a great fish that he had hooked while fishing with a live bunker off a Manasquan jetty one July morning.

He lobbed the bunker off the tip of the jetty into prime bass habitat. The bunker shot right back to his rock. Saunders again tossed the bunker back into the deep water and again the bait sprinted back into the rocks. The third time he threw the bait a huge swirl that he likened to a garbage can being pulled beneath the surface engulfed the bait and disappeared out of sight. A battle of major proportions ensued.

Tony Saunders was no stranger to monster bass. "I have been the bridesmaid, if you will, to many big fish," said Saunders. He witnessed Bill Daugherty's 53 pounder come a shore, he saw Steve Kean's 59 pounder the morning it was caught, and he was on the next jetty down when Mike Holowitz beached a 54 pounder. Tony, however, had never hooked into a 50 pounder on his own, and was well overdue when his time had finally come.

The hooked fish ran straight out "smoking" the reel, and it began thrashing violently on the surface. When the experienced bass man saw the fish he began to shake. "The fish was in control," remembered Saunders. The fish and Saunders went back and forth, to and fro across the tip of the jetty. The battle lasted upwards of 20 minutes. He finally had the fish fatigued and began working him to where he could beach it. He had it close enough to the jetty to where he could see the fish's great head. "Her eye was the size of a golf ball," said Saunders. "I could see the line coming out of her mouth, she was that close, and I knew the fish was a 60 pounder." Any surfcaster would die for a 50 pounder, let alone a 60. This was not just a fish of a lifetime, but rather a fish of many lifetimes.

Saunders being in what he felt was a good spot to land the fish decided it was time to bring the tired fish to his hand. He lifted the rod and directed the fish to where he was. It was at that moment that the hook finally let go and popped out of the fish's mouth. Saunders trophy slowly swam away. Despair overwhelmed him. He had to take three days off of work to try to cope with the loss, sleep was impossible and nightmares continue to this day.

It may sound strange, but this is typical of the passion and emotion that was commonplace in this pursuit of big bass.

Tony Saunders was one of a tight-knit group that pursued the mighty striper as hard as anyone possibly can. Working all day and fishing all night was the norm. Saunders and his cohorts would spend the night searching for and gathering bait to use on the jetties at dawn. The bait collection process was the secret to the success. He had places in the

Manasquan, Shark, Navesink and Shrewsbury Rivers and Sandy Hook Bay that he would visit nightly and he would always find the bunker. After catching them, either by snagging them with weighted treble hooks or by throw-netting them, he would then put the bunker into a 50-gallon tank with an aerator—a livewell in the back of his truck. When morning rolled around you would find him on one of the many Monmouth County jetty tips livelining his baits. It became an addiction to these guys more than a form of recreation. Obsession would be the best word to describe it.

The bunker stocks began to decline, in the mid 1980s, and they became harder and harder to get. This is when Saunders and good friend Steve Butelewicz, like others, began to get their bunker from the pound nets set-up in the Sandy Hook Bay. A few of the guys would carry a small aluminum boat on the top of their trucks; they were nicknamed "cartoppers." The small boat and engine enabled them to have access to productive waters at a moment's notice. They would throw the boat into the bay, shoot out to the pound nets, catch some bunker, thumbtack a $5 bill to a net post as compensation and then have the bait back in the live well in the truck in no time flat.

Saunders recalled a November night when he and Butelewicz launched Saunders's skiff from the beach at the Municipal Harbor in Highlands. It was at around midnight. The wind was blowing out of the northwest at 35 knots, which is not an unusual autumn wind in Jersey, but anyone with nautical experience will tell you this is a howling, dangerous wind for any boat, let alone a small aluminum boat. "The waves were high that night," recalls Saunders. "We were on our way back from the nets when a huge wave washed right over the boat swamping it." They bailed and tried for an hour to get the engine re-started without success. They were getting blown back towards the rock breakwater at the Harbor. As they approached the breakwater a huge wave lifted the boat and smashed it on the rocks splitting it wide open. "I thought we were dead," Saunders somberly admits. "I'm going Steve," he yelled. Both men jumped into the stormy froth and grabbed onto the rocks of the breakwater and waited for their impending doom.

By 6 a.m. they had pulled themselves up onto the breakwater, where, cold and shivering, they were finally rescued by an extensive Coast Guard operation using two boats, one to block the wind the other to rescue the men. In the ambulance they were put under space blankets and warmed.

Believe it or not, the very next night they were back out in Butelewicz' boat getting bunker from the pound nets once again!

Tony is just one example, one of many, who chased bunker and bass like no other. The kind of effort these guys put forth in order to successfully liveline was incredible. While this kind of effort is almost superhuman and not realistic for the common working man it was not done without good reason—livelining works!! As I said previously, great commitment produces great reward.

## GATHERING THE BAIT

The less pleasurable side of livelining is the collecting of the bait to use when "the big moment" arrives. It is a lot of work, but if you want to look at the bright side of it, I guess you can still consider it fishing, can't you? The bait you will collect is largely dependent on the season and what is available to you at the time. As an example, spring brings river herring; the warmer water then brings menhaden and juvenile bluefish, the autumn offers up mullet and juvenile menhaden (peanuts), the late autumn

*The Highlands Marina breakwater, where two men spent a November night figuring they met their match.*

sea herring and hickory shad. I would be remiss if I didn't mention the eel which can be used at any point throughout the season, but we'll talk about eels in detail in chapter 11. All of the gathering and fishing of bait of course must be done within the confines of local law.

The gathering of bait can be done in many different ways. You have to find the technique that works best for you in your locale. Once you capture a bait, it is then put into a bucket of fresh seawater for safe, healthy keeping until put into a livewell.

## WAYS TO CATCH VARIOUS BAITS

**Herring**—Herring can be caught by throw net but is more commonly caught by dart or Sabiki rig. When fishing a river where herring run, you can rig up a light-action rod and reel and attach a Sabiki rig with a 1-ounce sinker on the end. Cast out and up river letting the water sweep the rig while you reel slowly and jig with short jerks.

**Hickory shad**—Use the same technique as with herring using a Sabiki rig.

**Menhaden**—Menhaden can be snagged with a weighted treble hook or caught with a throw net when a pod is in close proximity.

The snagging with a treble is done by spotting a school, throwing a weighted treble across the school and then reeling quickly while sharply sweeping the rod to the side. (See Chapter 12 for more on snagging techniques).

Menhaden that have been snagged with the weighted treble and bleeding need to be kept out of the livewell until the penetration hole stops bleeding. The bunker needs to be put into a separate bucket of seawater until the bleeding stops and the bloody water needs to be changed frequently.

**Mullet**—Mullet are caught by throw net from the beach or bulkhead.

**Snapper (juvenile) bluefish**—Snappers are very aggressive and can be caught on small tin or by using a snapper popper.

**Scup/Porgies**—Caught with small pieces of clam or sandworm on size 4 or 6 Sproat or Virginia hooks. These fish can be caught around rockpiles and estuaries.

**Mackerel**—Macks are caught using small metal tins or teaser rigs that have small surgical tubing.

## KEEPING HEALTHY BAITS

Once you have caught your bait you then need to preserve it in the livewell until ready for use. There are stationary livewells and mobile livewells. I have heard of many different holding tanks, some quite comical, some inventive and creative, that have been used in the backyards, basements, and garages of bass men over the years. The list includes kiddy pools, goldfish ponds, bath tubs, garbage cans and swimming pools—if it can hold any amount of water it has probably been used. One of the best holding areas for live bait is the herring pen, but this requires access to open water at a dock where an angler can keep and access his bait as well as keep it secluded and safe from both thief and beast. The herring pen can hold large amounts of bait.

*A great way to collect fresh bait yourself is with a throw net. Here Gregg Oliver throws the net on a school of peanut bunker. They then go into an aerated 5-gallon bucket until fished later in the evening. Baits like peanut bunker and mullet can be found in the back bays, rivers and creeks in the early fall before the weather gets real cold.*

The most common livewell would be a 30- to 50-gallon tank with aerator. Custom-built tanks are common. They need to have a secure closable top, drain hose and good quality aerator. Livewells are commonly kept in the back of a vehicle where bait can be put after its capture and then transported to another place to either be fished or stored. Some use the vehicle livewell as their primary tank while others use it strictly as a means of transporting freshly caught baits to the fishing hole.

There are some very important things to remember about keeping your bait healthy and vibrant while in the livewell. Captain Alex Majewski from Lighthouse Sportfishing from Barnegat, New Jersey has done considerable research and writing on the livewell and I thought his words were well written and covers all the intricacies and "science" of livewell maintenance.

According to Captain Alex, *To successfully transport live bait, your bait tank's water quality must be properly managed. All you need is a basic understanding of dissolved oxygen, temperature and waste, and how these factors affect live bait. Remember to handle live baits carefully. You should not attempt to transport baits that have been dropped or are bleeding. If you do, you are almost guaranteeing that you do not pull out as many live fish from your tank as you put in. If at all possible, do not touch your baits during collection as this may remove some of their protective slime coating or even worse, scales. Round or oval tanks are best, as they prevent fish from continually hitting their noses in the corners.*

### Dissolved Oxygen

*It's a simple fact, fish need dissolved oxygen to breathe. Fish in a tank do not have an endless supply of oxygen, so the oxygen utilized by fish you are transporting must be replaced. Aerators and bait tank pumps are the most common ways of introducing oxygen and work by introducing atmospheric air, approximately 21 percent of which is oxygen, into the water. The Dayton or Challenger air piston pump and Keep Alive Oxygen Infuser are some of the most commonly used. These are 12-volt DC pumps that can either be wired directly to your car battery or to a dedicated bait pump battery. The amp draws are small enough that you don't have to worry about running your car battery down when operating the pumps for short periods with the engine off. Both the Challenger and Dayton pumps inject atmospheric air into the water via an air diffuser stone submerged in the tank. A lot of guys have switched over to pure oxygen injection from small tanks. (There are) no true mechanical parts and (this is) about the most effective way today of adding oxygen.*

*The volume of air pumped into the water will determine the amount of dis-solved oxygen available for the fish to breathe. More pumps are not always better, however, as they may increase the turbulence of the bait tank water to a point where the fish's physical exertion is increased. This increased physical exertion will increase the bait's oxygen consumption. One way of reducing your bait's oxygen consumption is by adding a fish tranquilizer, such as 'Tranquil' by Sure Life, to the water. Tranquilization reduces the physical activity of the bait, thereby reduc-ing the amount of oxygen needed. Tranquilizers also aid in reducing the stress as-sociated with transportation, thereby reducing fish injury and waste output.*

*Be mindful not to overstock your tank with baits. Overstocking will lead to rapid die off which may result in you getting to your spot with less baits than you would have if you had just put less bait in the tank to begin with. When collect-ing larger baits such as herring, my rule of thumb is one fish per gallon of water. Unfortunately, the number of baits you can transport in your set up may be best determined through trial and error.*

### Temperature

*The amount of dissolved oxygen water holds is directly related to temperature. The cooler the water the more dissolved oxygen it can hold. The warmer water is the less dissolved oxygen it can hold. In addition, your bait's oxygen consumption rate will increase with water temperature. The amount of oxygen a fish uses dou-bles with every 18-degree Fahrenheit water temperature increase. Logic would then dictate that you should cool your water down as much as possible prior to intro-ducing bait to your transport tank—this is not recommended. What I do recom-mend is trying to keep your tank water temperature stable and as close to the temperature of the water you are collecting bait from. If you do not, thermal shock may kill your baits. A rapid change in water temperature of only 5 degrees F can cause thermal shock. Be mindful as to where you keep your tank too, either while collecting or transporting bait. If your tank is in the back of an SUV or pick up truck with a cap, try to keep some windows open and park in the shade when load-ing up with bait. This will help reduce any effects the sun may have on heating up your vehicle—and the bait transport tank.*

*When I feel the need to cool my bait tank water down, or stabilize it, I add what I like to call "ice bombs". I use 2-liter plastic soda bottles filled with water and then frozen. I place several of these "ice bombs" in the tank while running heat-sensitive baits, such as herring, to my pen on warm days. You should not add ice directly to your water. If your ice was made with municipal water it is likely to contain chlorine. This chlorine will be released as the ice melts and can be deadly to the least sensitive live baits.*

*Waste*

*When fish are caught and then placed in a bait tank they immediately become stressed. In response to this stress, fish increase waste output, excess slime, and become very excited. The first sign of this stress is usually a noticeable clouding of the water. Although not directly caused by it, clouding of the water may indicate excessive ammonia build up. Ammonia is a product of fish waste and can be deadly if not controlled. Ammonia production usually peaks shortly after fish are caught and placed in a bait tank. There are several products available which aid in treating the ammonia.*

*The next noticeable problem associated with waste production may be foaming of the water. Foam prevents air from naturally dissolving into water, resulting in decreased dissolved oxygen levels. Antifoaming agents sold in many tackle shops reduce foam build up by breaking the surface tension of the foam causing it to go back into the tank's water. Remember that foam is a sign of stressed fish, so just decreasing the foam alone with chemicals may not increase the survival rate of your baits during transportation.*

*The easiest, most inexpensive way to control waste, foam, and ammonia build up is by flushing the tank water. I suggest replacing approximately 50% of the water before transporting your baits. Although partial water changes may eliminate the need to add chemicals, you should keep an eye on the water quality. You may want to add some chemicals anyway as a precautionary measure to treat waste that develops during transportation.*

## THE CHEMICAL LAB

The chemicals that you would need for your livewell care are available from "Sure Life." This company has been around for a long time; information on all of their chemicals can be found at *www.sure-life.com*. Here is a list of a few suggestions of chemicals that you may need for your livewell. You may have to get different products as situations arise.

- **Tranquil**—Is used to quiet the baits and help them "relax." This keeps the baits from becoming too stressed—remember stress is not good.
- **Foam-Off**—Helps remove foam that hinders oxygen from entering the water naturally.
- **No-Mmonia**—Helps remove chloramines and ammonia from water.
- **Sure-Life**—Is a water conditioner that removes chlorine from city water instantly.

- **Pogey/Menhaden Saver**—Made specially for mossbunker but also effective for mullet. Helps keep stress to a minimum and keep ammonia levels down.
- **Shad Keeper**—Made especially for blueback herring and shad. Helps fish not to get too stressed.

## FISH-PROVEN TACKLE AND RIGS

Now that we have covered bait preservation and transportation we now need to discuss what other equipment is needed for fishing the live bait. As far as rod and reel are concerned for livelining, there are several different set-ups, as usual. It will all come down to what feels comfortable for you. The standard rod size is usually an 8-to 9-foot conventional rod with fairly stiff action. Some liveliners have different rods for different baits. For example when fishing with herring they use lighter set-ups than when fishing with bunker, the reason being the strength of the rod needed for tossing a 2-pound menhaden is much greater than when throwing the much lighter herring.

The conventional reel is preferred for livelining and favorites include the Newell G229, Penn GS 525, Shimano Calcutta 400, Ambassador 7000 and the old standard Penn Squidder, which was used by many liveliners for a long time. Medium-size reels are lighter in weight, but still give you lots of line capacity. Since there are no long-distance casts when livelining, capacity is not a major concern but you do want enough for the long run when the fish of your dreams shows up.

The rig is very simple. You can tie the hook directly to the mono off of the reel, or off the mono leader if you are fishing with a braid line. The leader length comes down to what you feel is comfortable and wise. If you are jetty fishing you may want a heavier leader than you would use when fishing off of the beach. Mono leaders can range from 40 to 80-pound test.

The hook size depends on the size of the bait and how big the stripers are. I would go no smaller than a 4/0 and possibly go up to a 9/0. I prefer the Gamakatsu live bait hook. If you use a hook with an offset point, be sure that when you push the hook through the bait that the point angles out and away from the bait and not toward it.

Most liveliners use 20- to 25-pound test mono, or 50-pound Sufix Performance braid. Avoid lighter pound tests when using braid because there is not enough diameter in the line for when you need to grab the line with your fingers as you handle the line while working the bait.

A long-handle gaff will be needed if you fish from a jetty or bulkhead, and most liveliners make up their own gaffs at their home workshop. Some tackle shops also sell long-handle gaffs.

## LIVELINING TECHNIQUES

Livelining can be done off a jetty tip, bulkhead, bridge or an open beach. There are many variations and techniques that you can use most of which are relative to the exact location where you fish.

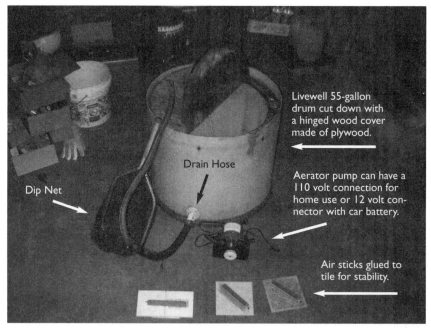

*The livewell. A lot of liveliners make there own livewells, and some good ones are available from retailers. A 30 to 50-gallon tank is adequate for transporting your live baits. A pan placed under your tank while in the truck will prevent spilled saltwater from stinking up your vehicle. Livewells need a good air pump to get the baits enough oxygen—here the bubble stick is glued to a ceramic tile to give it stability. A good drain is also important for when you get to your spot and need to put some water in the bucket before heading out. The drain also makes draining the tank an easy task. Don't forget your dip net, you will have a heck of a time trying to catch a bait without one.*

You need to have several livelining locations picked out ahead of time, and you need to make sure all your variables line up. Tidal stage would be one of those variables. You would be wasting a lot of time if you showed up at your jetty only to find no water because it is dead low tide. Rivers need to be targeted around the slack tides. Calm surf is also ideal for livelining. Big fish like calm surf. Make sure you have a good strategy planned.

Once you arrive to your target spot, you then remove a single bait from your livewell and put it into a 5-gallon bucket filled with enough water to handle the bait. You walk to the jetty, bridge or beach with the bucket.

When livelining you are presenting your live bait to the fish and you want to do it in a quiet uneventful manner, a natural presentation. The hook can be placed in the bait's back either in front of the dorsal fin or behind it between the fin and the tail. You want to catch enough meat of the fish to hold it, but not enough to mortally wound it, remember you are livelining, not dead-bait fishing.

Toss your bait out a short distance with a side-arm lob type of cast. The object is to get the fish out and away from you. You want to put it in deep water where the big fish hold and can home in on your bait. Your bait will either swim down and out, or back towards you. You want your bait to move away and run deep into the striper's line of vision. If it does this you are in good shape. If it swims back toward you, cast the bait out again.

When livelining you do so with the reel in free spool. As the bait swims, you let it take line. You'll get maximum sensitivity if you hold your line between your index finger and your thumb. This way you have a precision feel on what is happening down below. Once you feel the hit or take of the bait, wait a few seconds for the bass to turn the bait and mouth it, then put the reel into gear and set the hook—cross his eyes with a firm hook set.

I'm making this all sound simple, but it is a bit more involved and there will be different scenarios that unfold so you need to be flexible and adjust to what is happening. There are important intricacies that you will develop as you become more familiar with livelining, and in time you will learn the small tricks that master bass men use in order to get their bait to do what they want it to do. Most of the tricks are related to getting the bait deep in the water column, such as adding small sinkers to help convince the bait to stay down deep.

*While livelining you want to stay in careful contact with your line as the bait swims. Holding your line similar to the way it is held here will allow you to feel every move the live bait makes.*

So, there you have it, the information that you need to become a quality liveliner. There will be many small adjustments that you will make as you learn and as you develop your skills as a liveliner. The basic guide lines presented here are footholds to get you headed in the right direction. Mix in some experience and you will add another effective weapon to your striped bass arsenal.

# 11

# EELING STRATEGIES

The American eel, *Anguilla rostrata*, is commonly called a "snake" by surf fishermen. Eels are catadromous which means they live in fresh water and spawn in saltwater. The eel begins and ends its life in the waters of the Sargasso Sea, an area north of the Bahamas. A female eel can lay up to 4,000,000 eggs and often dies after doing so. After spawning and fertilization, the microscopic eggs hatch in nine to ten weeks, and in what seems like an impossible journey, they make their way back to freshwater rivers and streams to grow where the juvenile eels are called elvers.

Along the Atlantic Coast eels take up residence in areas like the Hudson River and Chesapeake Bay. They migrate far up into freshwater systems and may stay there for years, before heading back to the Sargasso Sea to spawn and die. They prefer to hunt by night. They lay low in mud, sand or gravel bottom areas, feeding on dead fish, insects, mollusks, crustaceans, worms and other fish.

While the eel is a slimy, ugly, snake-looking beast that takes some care to handle and needs to be literally wrestled onto your hook, one thing is notable; the darn things catch bass like mad. For the most part, if there are bass in the neighborhood and if you are fishing with an eel, a bass will probably end up on your hook.

Every good striper fisherman should be educated and well versed in how to fish eels and the numerous ways to use them to his advantage. I have seen them used in Hatteras at the Oregon Inlet Bridge and I have seen them used effectively as far north as Maine. My friend Mark Jolliffe has caught many a big bass on live eels from the Delaware River. They are a very reliable way to catch stripers anywhere and at anytime, and a big bass will not swim by one when offered.

## GETTING EELS

The fastest and easiest way to get eels is to pay a visit to your local tackle shop and buy some. For a regular session of a couple hours of surf fishing through a tide, I usually like to take six eels along; more for longer sessions.

Some surfcasters gather their own eels by using eel pots baited with some enticing food (for eels that is!) like horseshoe crabs, razor clams, herring, fish carcasses or crabs. The pot is then left overnight in a grassy marsh area or in a small creek somewhere and then checked the next day. Eel pots are handmade out of fine-mesh wire with nylon funnels sewn in them. The eels find their way into the pot to get the bait, but cannot find their way out because of the design of the funnel.

## TRANSPORTING EELS

You would not have to search very hard for a long list of different ways to transport eels. Most shops will bag your eels in a plastic bag with a little bit of water. If you bring a bucket, they will put your eels in it for you. From there you are on your own. Some fishermen take them direct to the striper grounds and then carry them around in either mesh bags that hang from the wader belt, or some use small soft cooler bags with a bit of sea weed. Some eelers keep small livewell coolers in their trucks to keep eels alive for long periods of time until needed.

*The livewell is a great way to keep your eels lively until you get out to the striper grounds. A livewell such as this one, used by surf guide Bill Wetzel, is very useful for the fisherman who fishes eels a lot. Bill usually carries more than one eel at a time mind you.*

**Double bucket system.** The double bucket system is a great way to keep your eels fresh and calm. A 2-gallon bucket with about 15 holes of ⅜-inch diameter drilled through the bottom, then placed inside a 5-gallon, bucket works very well. You must keep the smaller bucket off the bottom with a wooden block or a stone so that the ice melt and eel slime doesn't drown the eel. Place your eels in the smaller bucket and cover them with ice.

This system can be used for short-term storage up to a couple of days as long as they are kept chilled and the bucket drained. Keeping a lid on the 5-gallon bucket will also keep the eels at bay. This is a handy way to keep eels when you will be fishing and can keep the bucket nearby.

**Livewell.** For prolonged storage or when you fish eels on a regular or daily basis, a livewell can be used. A livewell can be kept in a garage or the back of a truck. There are many different styles of livewells; some are made easily at home, others purchased at your local tackle shop.

**Soft pack/cooler bag.** When transporting your eels to the striper grounds you can use a small soft-sided cooler pack or bag. By putting a cold pack in the bag along with a rag, the eels can be kept fresh and calm until ready for use.

**Mesh bag.** A mesh bag is used when you will physically be in the wash of the surf. It's not a long-term storage container; it's basically just for holding a few eels while you fish. The mesh bag is hung from the wader belt and eels are kept alive and frisky.

When wet suiting, the eels can be individually stored into a zip-type plastic bag with small holes in the bag and then put into your mesh bag. This way when you need an eel you just grab an individual bag, hook the eel and then pull the plastic bag off and store it in your plugbag to dispose of later.

## EEL-FISHING TECHNIQUES

Fishing with live eels is just downright fun. Not only do eels catch bass, but they also have the potential to take big bass. To me that's the fun! Many, many, many humungous bass have been taken on live eels in the surf. They are a natural enemy of the bass and an easy snack once the hungry striper finds one.

Fishing with eels in my experience has always been best in calm waters in the deep of night in a big-fish area. Although I suppose they would be effective in the daytime and I have seen them work with the lights on, the simple premise that big bass swim close to the beach at night is proof enough for me to fish them under the cover of darkness.

Fishing a live eel has to be one of the simplest ways to fish, not counting dealing with the squirming, slimy, annoying eel wanting to tie itself into an undoable knot while you're trying to get it onto the hook. I usually try to get my eel onto the hook without beating it senseless although sometimes you have to give it a whack against the bucket or a rock to make it calm down. I find that by not beating it, it stays fresh and spunky longer, and this is a good thing. I find that if I ice the eel down prior to usage that the chilling of the bait is enough to relax or sedate the little weasel.

The eel on the tag end of the line is retrieved similar to a swimmer only much, much slower. I reel my eel in only fast enough so that it cannot bury itself in a rock fortress causing me to get hung up. Yes it will fight you at times but just keep it moving slow and you will do fine. It's shaking to escape the hook you put through its nose, and this movement will work to your advantage by attracting bass to the area. By reeling extremely slowly you also allow the eel's scent to be carried off into the current calling bass into the vicinity. If conditions permit, I like to lift and drop the rod tip which makes the eel move up and down slightly in the water column perhaps giving a nearby bass a good look at the serpent in distress.

The basic eel rig is fairly simple. Tie a quality barrel swivel to the terminal end of the line using a Palomar knot, then add a length of 40- to 60-pound test monofilament, about 16 to 24 inches is about right. Tie a 6/0 to 8/0 short-shank tuna hook to the business end of the leader. I like the Gamakatsu Straight Eye Octopus Hook and I favor bigger hooks because I am a believer in being prepared for bigger fish. For casting from shore I have never used a weight on my eel rig. Eels naturally dive to the bottom anyway and sinkers can only get hung up between rocks. The weight of the eel is usually satisfactory to put the eel into the strike zone. If weight is needed, a small barrel sinker in front of the hook will get the job done.

There are several ways to skin a cat, or in this case, several ways to hook the eel. I have never brought it up to a science level—if the eel

*To hook an eel simply bring the hook up through the lower jaw and out through one of the eyes or the roof of the mouth. A rag is helpful with keeping control of the eel. I like mine between the eyes.*

stays on the hook and still swims, I am good with it. I bring the hook up through the bottom of the eel's chin and out between the eel's nose and eyes, right in the center.

## RIGGED EELS

When your live eel croaks, it's not useless—save it! Although the life is no longer in the eel it can still "live on" in a very productive manner, some would even argue it is more valuable dead than alive. We have been taught in our world today the importance of recycling. I don't think this is what the "suits" had in mind, but it's a good idea to recycle eels. Rigged eels and eel-skin plugs are a great way to re-use your eels after they have expired.

Fishing with rigged eels has always been a very reliable way to catch bass throughout the years. Bass men like the fact that you don't have to worry about trying to keep eels alive, and you don't have to deal with all the work that goes with that. Rigged eels are stored and ready at a moment's notice, all the preparation comes on the front side in the rigging process. Once called into action they are all ready to go, and after each use, if in good enough shape they're returned to the freezer or salt brine for future use.

Rigged eels can be kept in a salty brine or in the freezer. When freezing, they can be put into a plastic bag and stored, just remember to tell your wife they are there so that she is not freaked out when she cleans the freezer out. Another way to store them is by keeping them in a salty brine mix. When placed in the brine the eel will stay good for up to a year. The liquid brine is kept in a pickle-sized jar and is composed of water and a half box of kosher salt. After a fishing session, if the eel is not torn apart by a monster bass, it goes back into the brine until the next fishing session. The brine mix should be kept refrigerated in between fishing trips.

All the work of eel preparation is done long before you ever put your waders on. To rig an eel, you first have to have a dead one—of course! Then you have to decide which way to rig it: New Jersey style or New England style.

Most Jersey riggers use a block tin eel squid when prepping a swimming eel. There are different sizes and weights to provide different actions. The block tin eel squid is actually made up of a mix of 60/40 block tin and lead, which enables you to bend the keel on the squid to modify the swimming action. The angler's selection of the style of the eel squid gives him the ability to choose the tin that would work better in certain conditions. For example if you are fishing off of a deep hole on a jetty tip you would want your eel to run deep and you would use a narrow tin; however, if you are fishing a long shallow beach you don't need your eel to sink as deep and instead want a wider tin that will allow it to swim higher in the column. The eel squid you chose gives you the flexibility needed to cover different fishing situations. The eel squid also gives the surfcaster the ability to get the eel down deep into the striper's line of vision as well as increase the casting distance.

In New England the eel squid is not used at all. The eel is rigged in a similar fashion but without the squid head and no additional weight other than the slight amount added by the hooks and the Dacron. New Englanders tend to use bigger eels in this situation, big snakes of 15 to 20 inches in length.

I suspect the eel squid is not popular in New England primarily because it would hang up in much of the region's rocky bottom, whereas Jersey's bottom is almost completely sand and is thus very tin friendly.

## RIGGING NEW JERSEY STYLE

To rig an eel with a tin squid swimming head, you'll need the following materials.

- 12-inch rigging needle
- 50-pound Dacron braid, about 30 inches per eel
- Eel squid
- 6/0 Gamakatsu Live Bait Heavy Duty hooks
- Scissors
- Gudebrod Bait Rigging Floss, 35-pound test
- Cigarette lighter
- Zap-a-Gap glue
- Razor knife

*The completed New Jersey-style rigged eel.*

*The materials needed for rigging an eel Jersey style: 50-pound test Dacron, rigging needle, block tin eel squid, Gudebrod Bait rigging floss (35-pound test), 6/0 Gamakatsu Live Bait Heavy Duty hooks, Zap-A-Gap and cigarette lighter.*

The best size eels for Jersey rigging are 10 to 12 inches in length, and skinnier eels have better action than heavier, fat eels.

Before you start, grab the head and the tail of the eel and pull, you will hear the cracking of the spine. You do this to be sure the eel is straight and will not finish with a humpback after rigging.

1—Double over a 30-inch length of Dacron and run the loop through the eye of the rigging needle with about 2 inches outside the needle eye.

2—Slide the needle into the mouth of the eel, run it through the body and out about a half inch past the vent. Remove needle from the Dacron then pull out about 6 inches more Dacron.

3—Attach a 6/0 hook to the Dacron by tying a barrel knot. (Slide loop through the eye of the hook bring it out, open the loop, give the hook a half turn and then put the loop back over the bend of the hook, then repeat but twist the loop the opposite direction, then one more time

*This is what the barrel knot looks like just before it gets cinched tight.*

reversing the direction again. Then thread hook through loop and pull loop up to where the line enters the eye of the hook, then slowly pull knot tight. It will look similar to picture if you did it correctly).

4—After tying the barrel knot, grab the two tag ends coming out of the eel's mouth and pull, sliding the hook up snug up into the eel's body. Seat the hook where the bend begins, leaving only the bend of the hook and point protruding (see picture).

*The rear hook completed. Make sure all knots are snug but not too tight as to cut through the skin of the eel.*

5—Take your rigging floss and cut three 10-inch lengths. These will be used to secure the trailer hook firmly and hold it into place. Tie one strand in front of the eye of the hook, one just behind the eye of the hook and one at the bend in the hook. To tie off, use a double overhand knot followed by two single overhand knots. Tie these knots securely and firmly.

6—Next you will need to figure out the squid placement by holding the squid alongside the eel. Figure on leaving roughly ¼ to ⅜ inch between the nose of the eel and the eye on the squid. You will now run the hook up through the eel just behind the gills or pectoral fins and out the top of the eel. Note: Take care not to hit the spine or the Dacron line holding the tail hook.

7—Next you will actually tie the eel to the hook three different times again using the floss. This is done first by tying your line to the hook using a double overhand knot followed by two overhand knots at position (A), then you wrap the line around to the top of the eel's head (B), tie it off to the eel first and then to the hook again with double overhand and then around to the bottom (C), again tie the eel and then the hook using another double overhand knot and the two single overhand knots to finish it off. This will hold the head of the eel in place. Remember the exact placement is important.

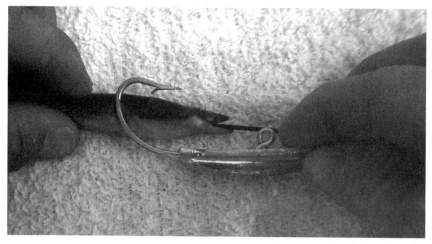

*The placement of the eel squid is important. Carefully plan its position. You want the nose of the eel within about ¼-inch of the eye, with enough room to tie off the knots.*

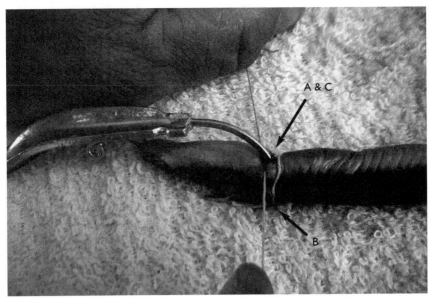

*You are actually going to tie the eel to the hook three times in this step. A, B, and C mark the positions where these double overhand knots will be tied. The positioning is critical so chose your location carefully.*

8—Next we will tie the mouth of the eel closed, again using floss. Simply tie the mouth shut using one double and two overhand knots.

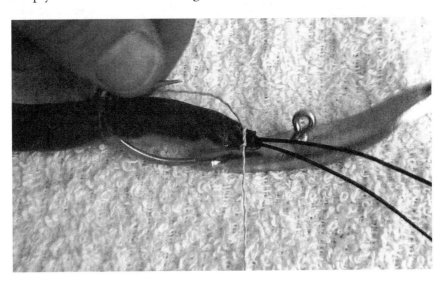

*The mouth of the eel is tied shut with floss.*

9—You will now tie the Dacron to the hook eye on the eel squid. Do this by using a surgeon's loop knot. This knot is critical because it creates tension from the hook bend to the eel squid. If this knot slips and loosens it will cause the squid to swim erratically or (worse) straight. Next we need to finish securing the head of the eel, this is done by taking the two remaining tag ends of the Dacron and running them both through the hook eye of the squid only they will each go through the eye in opposite directions. Bring the ends back towards the eel and run them again crisscross below the Dacron and eel tied end three times creating a surgeon's knot, slowly cinch the knot tight. It is at this point that you will need to create the proper tension before you finalize your knots. This needs to be tight but not too tight as to cause a "humpback" at the middle of the eel. It is at this point that you will need to make sure that the eel is set at the proper distance from the eye so that it does not sit bunched up, or crooked or loose. Once you have it set to where you want it, finish off your knot with a double and two single overhand knots.

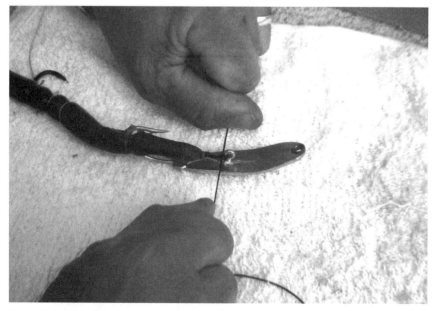

*You will tie off the Dacron to the eel squid using a surgeon's loop knot. This final tie-off is critical. Be sure the placement is in a "natural" position before finalizing the knot.*

*The final tie-off completes the task. Cut the long ends and Zap-A-Gap the knot or put a flame to it to seal the deal.*

10—Finish by sealing the knot with a shot of Zap-A-Gap or similar glue, or you can sear the tag ends with a cigarette lighter or both.

That's it, you're done! Time to go fishing.

## RIGGING EELS NEW ENGLAND STYLE

This technique was shown to me by Pat Abate at River's End Bait and Tackle in Connecticut. I'll tell you what, I surely wasn't the first one he has shown how to rig eels, and I am sure there is a long list of predecessors that came before me. He is one of the East Coast's top eel riggers. While with him, I also got a glance at his coveted and protected container of eel skins which he never lets out of his sight for even a minute.

*The completed New England style rigged eel. Notice there is no eel squid.*

Materials needed for this process are the same as New Jersey style except you will not need the swimming squid heads, since the New England style does not use them.

1—Repeat steps 1 through 4 above only this time using 7/0 Owner Cutting Point hooks.

2—Once you have the rear hook set in position you will then secure it so that it does not move. This is done by using the floss and needle. In a crisscross pattern you want to come into the eel's body at an angle, go through the eel and the eye of the hook and come out on the other side of the eel at the same angle. (See photo). You do this in both directions creating an "X". You then repeat the same steps on the opposite side of the eel. Complete each side by tying off tag ends using the same overhand knots as described above. Remember, do not tie too tight or you will cut into the eel skin. This cross pattern will keep the hook extremely stable.

3—We now move on to the front hook. First you want to stick the hook point into the mouth of the eel and bring it out the bottom of the eel behind its skull being careful not to hit your Dacron and keeping it centered. You want the tip or the lips of the eel to fall just behind the eye of the hook.

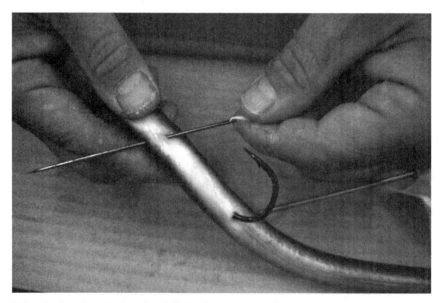

*Bring the floss through the eel and the hook eye at an angle.*

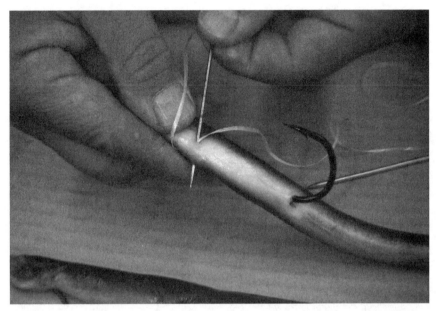

Here you will come around the eel and go back through at a 90-degree angle creating an "X" pattern. Repeat on the other side and you will stabilize the rear hook and keep it from rolling left or right.

Here you see the front hook placement. Be careful not to catch your Dacron or the eel's spine when you go through.

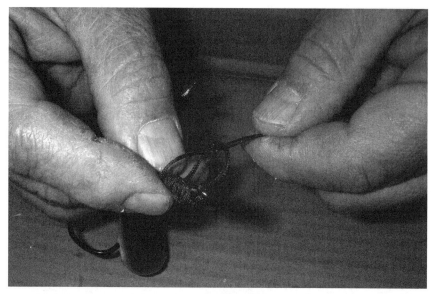

*Half hitches up the shank of the hook get hit with Zap-A-Gap to provide a good base for the eel once it's slid into position.*

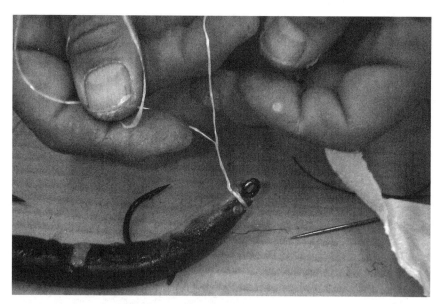

*Your final step will be tying the mouth of the eel closed on top of another good dose of Zap-A-Gap. Your eel is now ready for a meeting with a cow.*

4—You now want to bring your Dacron end back through the eye of the hook and run half hitches down the shaft of the hook at least ¾ of an inch. Seal this series of half-hitches with a good dose of Zap-A-Gap or other super glue. You will then bring the eel up to its final resting place. You will now tie the mouth closed and onto the shank of the hook just short of the eye. You will need to tie this off with floss by doubling the floss and creating a loop, run the loop over the lips of the eel. Then take the two tag ends and finish them by tying double overhand knots. Cut off the tag ends, Zap the knot and you are ready for some exciting striper fishing.

## EEL-SHIN PLUGS

The eel-skin plug has the ability to take fish when no other plugs will. If you need convincing, just ask someone who has used one; I'm sure anyone who has seriously fished a skin plug is a true believer. The work involved with the skinning of an eel and the dressing of the plug with a skin may deter some fishermen, but the actual usage and success will keep you coming back for more.

Skinning the eel is a relatively quick and easy process. For eel skin plugs you will want a pretty good size eel, about a 24-inch length, as eel skins do not have a lot of stretch in them. A good size skin-plug eel would be one at least 24 inches in length for proper diameter to fit over a standard wood plug. You will need a razor blade or knife, and a pair of pliers.

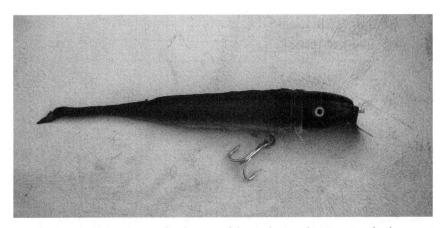

*The eel skin plug has to be considered as one of the top bass catchers in striper land.*

Start by cutting a ring around the neck of the eel just behind the pectoral fins. Do not cut it too deep, just deep enough to cut through the skin. Peel back the skin far enough to grab a piece of it with the pliers. Once you get an area of skin, you just peel the skin off the eel with a long steady pull. You will then have an eel skin hanging from your pliers. When skinning larger eels you may want to secure the head so you get a better pull; some nail it to a post and then work the skin off carefully.

You can use the skin with the inside out, which is favored by some because of its silvery bluish tint, or turn it back so the outside is once again on the outside. The skin should be soaked in a salty brine solution for several days, using the same type of solution you made for rigged eels with kosher salt. Keep the skins and the brine solution in the refrigerator.

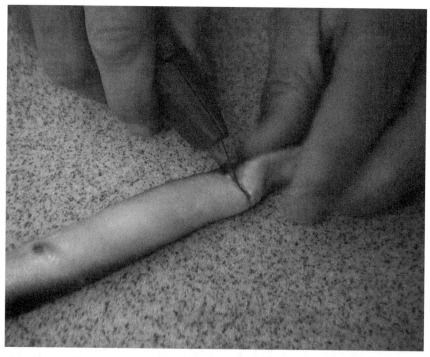

*To begin the skinning process cut a ring around the eel neck only deep enough to cut the skin. You don't want to cut the head off.*

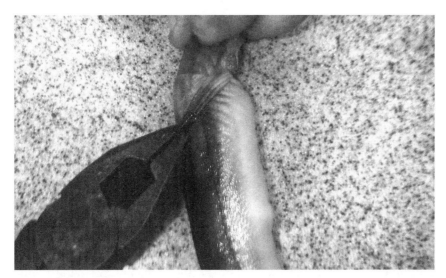

*Grab a piece of skin with pliers and slowly pull it down towards the tail. Be careful not to peel any flesh off with the skin especially near the anal vent.*

## DRESSING THE EEL-SKIN PLUG

There are a few things to keep in mind as you get ready to put the skin on a plug. First make sure your skin is wide enough (diameter) to fit over the plug, and you also want to check it for length. I like a tail long enough so that it will flutter tantalizingly and tease a big girl into striking, but it can't be too long so that it doubles back and hangs up on the plug's hooks.

*Carefully slide the skin onto the plug. If you force it or if the skin is not wide enough to fit over the plug you will rip the seam of the eel skin.*

The plug in this example is a wooden metal-lip swimmer manufactured by Afterhours Custom Plugs. The plug you use should have a groove cut behind the eye or just behind the lip that goes all the way around the circumference of the plug. This will hold the rigging floss used to tie the skin in place. Remove the existing hooks from the plug, unless you want to leave the tail hook on. The tail hook can work to your advantage by keeping the tail from swinging forward on the cast. Some also opt to use a heavy monofilament loop off the back wire of the plug. Weed whacker line works great! As usual it comes down to your preference about what you want to do. And, remember to experiment.

Carefully slide the skin onto the plug and tie it in place using rigging floss. Make sure the "seams" of the eel skin are at the top and bottom (you'll see the fine lines on the eel's skin that look like a seam). The bottom seam will lie right across the plug's hook hangers or swivels on the bottom of the lure. Tie the skin on by starting at the bottom, tying a double overhand knot, going half way around the plug to the top tying another double overhand knot, and then go back to the bottom tie a third double overhand, followed by two single overhand knots to finish. Trim off the extra floss and then seal it with a drop of Zap-A-Gap.

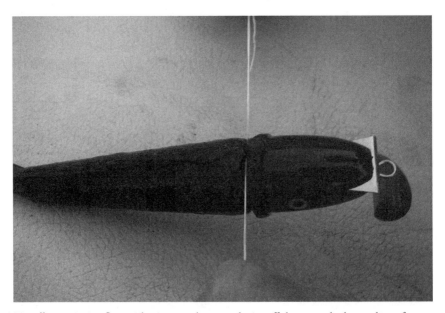

*Tie off your rigging floss with nice snug knots and trim off the tag ends then a drop of Zap-A-Gap to seal the deal.*

Next, you will then need to cut a small hole for the front hook hanger or swivel to come through (an X-Acto knife works great here). Cut a small slot perpendicular to the plug's length, not with it, so the skin will not tear nearly as easy when a big bass is sucking on the tail. Place a split ring and a treble hook on the eye of the swivel, usually a 2/0 to 4/0 size. The hook should match up and balance with the size of the plug, so you'll have to figure out what size hook works best for your particular plug. One of the best treble hooks is the Eagle Claw Beak style with the hook points that bend slightly inward. These hooks won't dig into the skin.

As mentioned above, you may also want to include a rear single hook. It is considered a good hook if for nothing else than keeping the tail skin from doubling back and getting hung up on the front hook during the cast. I like a single 6/0 Siwash as the rear hook and this accounts for a good number bass in the same way the rear hook on the Slug-Go takes its share of short-hitting fish.

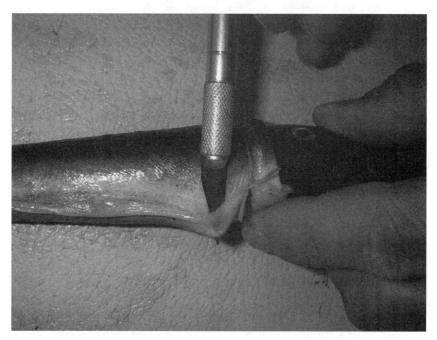

*Carefully cut a small hole just big enough to get the plug's swivel through then add a split ring and hook, and you will be ready to fish!*

Although I used a wooden metal-lip plug here, there are many other lures, plastic or wood, that also wear skins very well. I have played around with dressing a few others including the Bomber, I guess it smelled good because a couple of bass liked it, but it swam terribly. It's also wise to dress needlefish with eel skins. I have used the Gibb's stubby needle in the past with reasonable success and Gibb's big needle is also deadly when dressed with a skin.

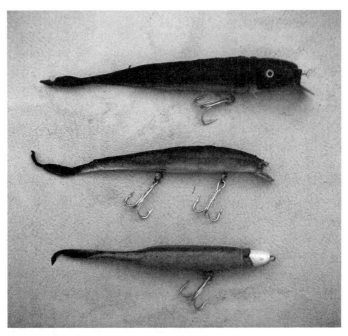

*Here are three different eel-skin plugs; top to bottom, Afterhours plug, a Bomber, and a Gibb's stubby needle. As an experiment I "skinned" a Bomber, it swam poorly with limited action but the bass seemed to like it anyway. Don't be afraid to experiment!*

# 12
# SNAG-AND-DROP STRATEGIES

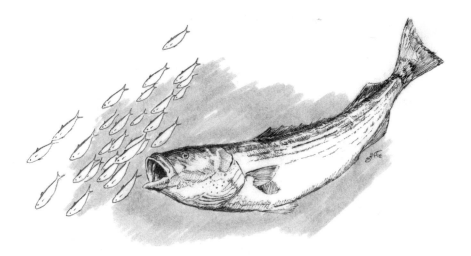

When the mossbunker come to town they always have a way of sprucing up the action. Why? Simply because bass absolutely love them!

Back in Chapter 10 we talked about livelining techniques. Now it's time to discuss a unique variation of livelining called the snag-and-drop technique. This is a different type of livelining technique that every surfcaster should be well versed in. It's a viable way to take bass, especially at those times when bass want nothing but the real thing. An added benefit of snag-and-drop is that you don't need to have a livewell full of ready baits.

Snag-and-drop opportunities usually occur at a time when you don't expect something to happen. You can't plan where the bunker schools will be from day to day. The difference between livelining and snag and drop is that livelining is a calculated well-made plan, whereas snag-and-drop usually happens as a bait situation unfolds in front of you. Being prepared and knowing what to do when the bunker ball up in front of you could mean the difference between a nice linesider lying at your feet, or driving home with a smelly old skunk in the back seat.

Sure it is fun to take bass on artificial lures, but when the bait comes close to you, you have to strongly consider using live bait especially when the bait is adult bunker. Adult bunker give you one of your best possible chances at hitting a fish of a lifetime. Being prepared when a situation presents itself is essential.

As a side note, I have been asked many a times why I don't try to snag-and-drop sea herring in the fall, the same way we snag bunker. My answer is that I have, but the herring are much quicker than the clumsy bunker, thus making them very hard to snag. The bunker are so tightly schooled you would have a hard time *not* snagging one if your cast landed in the right place.

## UNDERSTANDING BUNKER

By understanding how bunker move, how they school and how they react to different situations will help you make better decisions when they are in front of you. I have talked to my two diver pals, Art Nelson and Mike Laptew, about what bunker schools do beneath the surface; what we as beach fishermen can't see, and they both mention similar patterns.

The bunker travel in large schools cruising along doing their filter-feeding thing. When some bass show up, the bunker get nervous and start balling up for protection, this is what we see when the surface of the water gets very dark and the bunker are so tightly balled that some are actually getting pushed up and out of the water. Several bass will then charge through the school while the others continue to circle the perimeter. As soon as the school is penetrated and broken up, the perimeter bass chase and eat everything that moves away from the pod. That sounds about right!

To shed more light on the scenario I want to share with you a day when I found a school of peanut bunker on the beach. The school and I were alone, and there was no outside, unnatural factors impacting the situation. These fish were able to do what they do naturally without human interference. There were no fishermen casting lures into the school or around it. Since I was alone I decided to observe the situation for a little while rather than indulge in it.

*It was a school such as this I found one day. I realized that it was time to study in nature's classroom. When you happen across a school of peanut bunker such as this, good things await you. If the school isn't "active" be patient and sooner or later some bass will show up. Bunker and bass are a natural combination.*

This particular bunker school was easy to see in the flat, clear afternoon water. The school was roughly 30 yards long and about 8 feet wide. The interaction between the peanuts and the bass was cool to watch. The peanuts would spread out in the trough and travel in a relatively long thin line. They would then begin to get uneasy and start to ball up. The school would transform from long and brownish line into a round and black, almost purple, ball. They then began to get very nervous and fluttery, some to the point of flipping far out of the water as if they got thrown into the air by the group below. Then abruptly the bass would blitz the school running through it smashing it apart for a few seconds.

The bass blitz was followed by some uneasiness, but when things quieted down, the bunker spread out and again began to swim happily down the shore line like nothing happened. A few minutes later they would again repeat the previous act; ball up, get attacked and then spread out again like nothing happened. This went on for a long period of time, I watched for 20 minutes to a half hour studying everything. Believe me it was hard not to cast to these fish.

After watching this similar pattern over and over, I then decided it was time to inject some human interaction, but I wanted to do it with calculated and carefully timed casts. I wanted to cast at particular times and watch if and when and what the fish would do based on my timed casts.

I broke my timed casts into three categories; quiet time, blitz time, and post-blitz time. I wanted to see if it mattered when I cast. First I tried casting my small 3-inch metal-lip swimmer into the quiet "happy" school and to the area around the school. Nothing happened, no real surprise, the bunker just cleared a path and let my swimmer pass through. Then I waited for "blitz time" when the bass blitzed the school, and I threw the small metal-lip swimmer among the breaking, rolling fish, right into the center of the action as if my lure was one of the fleeing peanuts. Believe it or not I got no hits while the blitz was on, and this surprised me. I did this repeatedly with no result. Next I waited for the post-blitz period following the bass assault and cast my lure behind the school, beyond the school and in front of the school, and I had bass on nearly every cast. I then waited for the bunker to return to happy mode and cast a few around the area, and caught nothing. I had figured out a definite pattern.

To summarize my observations, what I saw coincided with what Laptew and Nelson told me. The peanuts moved happily down the beach, then the bass showed up and began circling the school balling it up. The bass would then attack the school breaking it up or fragmenting it. Once fragmented, the bass worked as individuals attacking and consuming stray peanuts that had broken away or separated from the main bunker school. It all made perfect sense.

This situation helped me to understand the predator-prey relationship between the bunker and bass, which I wanted to share with you. The same situation happens when adult bunker show, only all the players are much bigger.

Let's talk about the snag-and-drop technique. Some important things that you will need to do whenever you come within close proximity of bunker schools, adult or juvenile, is to first recognize what is happening; and second, you will need to be prepared with the proper rig and equipment. Lastly you will have to act quickly, every second counts when these quick-moving fish show up at your front door. Bunker move very fast at times.

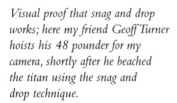

*Visual proof that snag and drop works; here my friend Geoff Turner hoists his 48 pounder for my camera, shortly after he beached the titan using the snag and drop technique.*

## SNAG-AND-DROP TECHNIQUES

When the rare and golden opportunity of adult bunker schooling up and balling up in front of you occurs, consider yourself extremely lucky because the golden goose just laid the golden egg right on your foot. You need to move quickly into action, especially if the school is "active" or "hot." A hot pod of big bunker has big bass blowing up all through it. It is, in my estimation, the best, most exciting, sight that a surfcaster can see. This is the perfect time and situation for you to get the biggest bass you ever caught—a real wall hanger. When you have big bass on big bait on the feed your chances are just great provided you do the right thing and react wisely.

An artificial-lure purist might say, "I'll put on a big popper or big wood swimmer!" I say in return "Why would you want to do that? Do you want to catch the small bass on top? The 20 and 30 pounders?" The big bass hang down deep and are less aggressive, but smarter and just as hungry, only they just wait for the fallout to come down to them. While the small bass race around on the surface, big ones hang below the bait waiting for an offering to drop down to them. This is where snag and drop is the perfect card to play because once you snag and drop the bait, it will be right in the face of those bass that are truly large!

Keep in mind that big bunker move quickly and at times disappear just as fast as they appear. Sometimes they move so fast you will only get one shot at a school. At other times the school may hold in front of you for quite a long time, perhaps with bass sitting on the perimeter, perhaps no bass at all. There is no way that you can really tell for sure, so you have to offer them something—just give it a try.

Last season while fishing a jetty, a huge school of bunker suddenly appeared and heading directly towards the jetty I was on. My buddies and I thought for sure we were going to hit some good fish. The school came right to us, two of us snag-and-dropped while the other pencil poppered the perimeter. For 20 minutes we fished hard, and waited with high expectations until the school finally took off. Needless to say we were disappointed because the school either had no bass or the bass were off the feed, either way it was a bit frustrating, but that's bunker for you. You always hear about the victories in the surf, nobody wants to mention the losses, but they happen a lot. They're all part of the game!

## THE SNAG-AND-DROP RIGS

There are basically three snag and drop rigs that I use, each one slightly different and used in different situations or scenarios. At the very least, you have to have the weighted treble ready to go, then one of the other two also at hand. This way you'll be ready when the bunker appear.

**Rig #1**—This is the weighted treble hook. When big bunker are likely to be present I carry either a 10/0 or a 12/0 weighted treble at all times. I can get this out of my surfbag quickly and have it attached to my line within a few seconds, about as long as it would take me to switch a lure. I use this when the bunker are right in front of me within easy casting distance. This weighted treble can cast about 60 to 70 yards.

**Rig #2**—This rig is tied with heavy monofilament leader material, 80 or 100 pound test. On one end you will tie a barrel

*The weighted treble hook (a.k.a. bunker snagger) is a plug bag must when big bunker are a possibility. You can attach one of these to your business end quickly resulting in the fish of your dreams—maybe even bigger.*

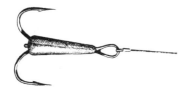

*Rig #1—The weighted treble or snatch hook or bunker snagger. A 10/0 or 12/0 size should be "at the ready" whenever adult menhaden swim nearby.*

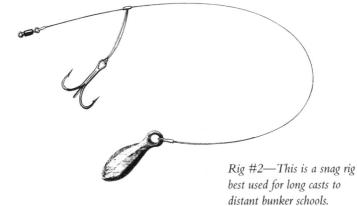

*Rig #2—This is a snag rig best used for long casts to distant bunker schools.*

swivel. Then you will tie a dropper loop that will hold a 5/0 VMC treble hook. The remaining tag end will have a loop tied to the bottom, roughly 10 inches down from the dropper loop. On the bottom loop you put a 3- or 4-ounce bank sinker. This is a great rig for distance.

**Rig #3**—The last rig is a larger version of the rig we use for snagging peanut bunker. It starts with a barrel swivel, an 8-inch length of mono holding a 3- or 4-ounce barrel or egg sinker then another barrel swivel, followed by a second 80- to 100-pound leader about 12-inches long and finished off with a 4/0 or 5/0 treble hook. This is a versatile rig that can be used for long distances or short distances, although it won't cast quite as far as rig number two.

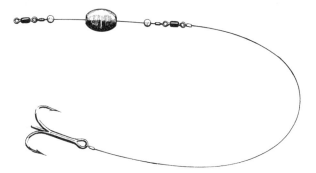

*Rig #3—Snag rig for adult bunker. A 3- to 4-ounce egg sinker gives good casting distance and good sinkability.*

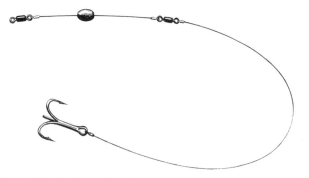

*Rig#3 (modified)—Peanut bunker snag rig. A scaled-down version of the rig used for adult bunker. Use a ¼ to 1-ounce egg sinker with a 3/0 VMC treble hook, and a total rig length of about 12 to 14 inches.*

With a school of bunker in front of you, you want to cast the rig be-yond the school of bunker and give it a short time to sink, probably around three seconds. If you got off a good cast you will feel your line hitting the bunker (kind of a bump, bump sensation) as the rig drops through the school. When you start feeling those little bumps of the bunker start re-trieving quickly while jerking back hard on the rod in a sweeping side-ways motion. Once you hit a bunker you will know it immediately. You will feel like you have a small bluefish on your line and the vibration of the hooked bunker on the business end of the line will be obvious.

At this time stop reeling. Don't open the bail, but just let the bunker drop below the school. Let the weight of the rig pull the bait down to the bottom. Stay in touch with your bunker the entire time by keeping a slack-free line.

Once you have done this the waiting game begins. You will feel the bunker vibrate trying to swim free. Concentrate on that feeling and be aware of any changes. When the vibrating ceases, it means one of two things happened; one bad, one good. The bad means that the bunker may have freed itself and shook off the hook. Check this with a few quick

*After spotting a school of adult bunker near the beach cast out, snag a bunker using one of the three rigs shown. Let it sink and hold on. Andy Schmidt battles a contender.*

cranks on the reel and then lift the rod. If it feels light, the game is over, hit the "reset button" by casting over the school again to snag another bunker.

The good option is that your bunker stopped vibrating because a humongous bass just inhaled the darn thing, pulverized it and it's now in the bass' gullet. I like to wait a few seconds to give the bass time to get that pogie down the hatch a little further. It may sound weird but I try to visualize what is happening in the bass-bunker relationship. Once I feel the hook is well inside the mouth of the fish, I then reel up all slack quickly, point the rod at the fish (bow to the cow as Alberto Knie puts it), and then come back extremely fast and hard with the rod. You want to embed the hook into something hard or deep. I will usually hit a big bass three times total to be sure the hook is set, but not so much so that I open a hole so the hook can fall out. From there on a classic battle will ensue—have fun!

*Schmidt wins the battle with a nice striper on the beach, snag and drop at its finest.*

## WHAT ELSE CAN HAPPEN?

Now what I just described to you is an ideal textbook execution, if you will. I made it sound simple and I did it in "slow motion" for you. In real life the entire scenario will unfold and be over within seconds. Sometimes weird and unpredictable things happen. You need to forever be ready for whatever the surf gods throw in your direction. I will give you this one hint, there will be a lot of curves. Let's take a look at what might happen.

Every once in a while you will feel the take and then your line will start running left or right at a high rate of speed. This happened to me one summer morning as I snagged a bunker straight out off my jetty a good distance from me perhaps close to 100 yards. I felt the pick up and then watched as the line went from 12 o'clock in front of me to 3 o'clock off to my right, and it happened within seconds! I reeled quickly and finally caught up to the fish. The line finally came tight and I hit it hard. The fish was almost behind me by then, but after a battle, I finally landed a 28 pounder. I felt rather lucky because I had no control until late in the game.

Sometimes the fish will take the bait and then may make a run straight at you. Thinking your bait got off, you may be surprised when you find out the bass is still on and only 20 feet in front of you. If your line goes slack be 100 percent sure that the bunker is really gone before you give up. This may mean reeling in at 3000 rpms to catch up to your rig.

Don't be fooled into thinking that monster bass won't come in extremely close to the beach. I have seen huge fish in the wash eating discarded bunkers or bunker heads, like a cop in a doughnut shop.

Another option if the bunker and bass are close to the beach is to reel your bunker in all the way and take the time to re-hook it firmly, then cast it out. Some guys change to a single hook, but I never wanted to waste time doing that so I just re-set the hook in a better spot such as the back of neck or behind dorsal fin and lob it back out. Note: Make sure your rod is capable of lobbing a 2-pound bunker 20 or 30 yards. You won't catch anything with a broken rod!

Big bunker and big bass call for big equipment when snagging-and-dropping. You will need a high-capacity reel such as a Penn 704 or 706 Z, or a Van Staal 200, 250, 275, or 300 loaded with 50-pound Sufix braid. You will need a long powerful rod, say 10 to 11 feet, and rated to handle 4 to 6 ounces. I like the Lamiglas XS101MS factory rod and either the GSB-120-1L or GSB-132-1L custom blanks. Another favorite for this situation is the 10-foot, 6-inch All-Star 1267-2 custom rod.

## PEANUT BUNKER SNAG-AND-DROP TECHNIQUES

One thing most East Coast surfcasters can count on each fall is a sustained run of juvenile menhaden, nicknamed peanut bunker. They usually run about 3 inches in length, although I have seen them as small as only 1-inch long and as big as 6 inches. I am not sure why they call them peanut bunker, they don't look like peanuts—all I can guess is that the bass snack on them like humans eating peanuts at a baseball game.

Anyway they really crank up the surf action as millions of them migrate along our beaches. They travel in large schools and when the water is flat and clear they like to run very close to the shoreline in the drop-off. They stay close to the beach when the wind is blowing off the beach because bunker always have to swim into the wind.

They are very easy to spot as the pods look like huge dark stains in the water and they flicker on the surf as though someone was throwing small pebbles. When they are in the skinny water along the beach they become very easy and irresistible targets for bass, and also for bluefish, to trap and assault, and that makes it easy for the surf guys to get some work done.

Of course peanut bunker offer the surfcaster countless options in approach and bass can be caught on a plethora of artificials, but at times the bass become finicky opting only for the real thing. One tried-and-true method, especially when bass get fussy is to snag and drop peanuts to bass waiting below or around the bunker school.

The rig to snag peanuts is similar to rig number three on page 166 for adult-size bunker, only scaled down so everything is smaller and lighter. I start with a barrel swivel tied to a 6-inch length of 40-pound mono with a ¼- to 1-ounce egg sinker slipped on, then tie on another barrel swivel, to which is tied a 40- to 100-pound test (100-pound if blues are in the mix) leader with a 2/0 or 3/0 VMC treble hook at the end. It's a good idea to crush the barbs down to minimize injury to the bass. If fishing is good and the peanuts bigger in size, I will go with a single 6/0 or larger hook to reduce gut-hooking the bass and to simplify unhooking fish.

Cast over the school of peanuts, wait a few seconds then stroke back on the rod sideways, but not too hard, especially if you are using braid and a graphite rod—you will end up ripping the little bunker in half. With this set-up, jerk back with a little more ease than you would when snagging adult bunker.

*When you find a peanut bunker school with bass blowing up on them yet you are having trouble with hooking up, a snag-and-drop rig will usually get the job done. Tie up a couple of rigs and keep them in your plug bag for when the opportunity arises.*

When you hook a 'nut, let it drop, then wait for a hard hit similar to the hit of a lure. Once you feel it, give the bass a few seconds to mouth the bait or wait until the bass runs and your line goes tight, then hit the fish. Sound easy? It isn't that hard.

A 7- to 9-foot rod works well for snag-and-drop with peanut bunker. When bass are on the smaller side, 34 inches and less, scale down on the size of the tackle so the fight is more sporty and lightweight. Hey, when the bass are smaller and very close to the beach why not? I prefer a rod like a 7-foot St. Croix that has some muscle yet it's still soft.

I've found that high modulus graphite rods accompanied with braid line are not good for snagging peanuts. The lack of stretch or give of any kind rips the hook right through the baby bunker (notice the tear in the peanut in the photo above). To offset the problem either go with a softer rod or make the adjustment on your rod sweep to shorter, gentler strokes.

Snag-and-drop is fun, so you can enjoy the time doing it. Of course when bunker bring the big fish rolling through it's exciting. Try to relax, don't panic and you will have better success. This technique may bring you as close as you will come to the cow of a lifetime.

# 13

# THE WRAP UP

The season of the bass is in constant flux and changes continually. The tuned in surfcaster takes advantage of the changing opportunities and uses various strategies and techniques to stay in synch with the bass. By being flexible and familiar with all of the lure and bait techniques, you can change and alter your strategy to take bass with whatever technique works.

For example, in my home waters of Jersey, surfcasters greet the new season in March and April by fishing worms and clams for early run bass in the backwaters of the bays. Come April and May we start collecting herring from the Delaware River to liveline in the rivers and local canal. In June the big bunker show up, and I like to chunk with bunker heads and throw big artificials like 4-ounce pencil poppers and big metal-lip swimmers for large stripers. Big bunker also make for great livelining and snag-and-drop fishing. Once the big bass move north, the summer patterns set in, and we start raking crabs and fishing small artificials for summer bass. Come September, the mullet run emphasizes top-water plugs like poppers and metal-lip swimmers, and by October the primary bait is peanuts. The rough surf of the hurricane season demands clam fishing. November brings sand eels and red-hot migration fishing on artificials. Ah yes and then there are the eels, good just about anytime and anywhere bass swim.

There are hundreds of ways, maybe thousands of techniques and strategies, used to catch a striped bass. As a surf man you can be told exactly what to do with very specific instructions about how to catch fish, and you can read all the books and all the magazine articles ever written, but in the end it will be you alone that needs to develop your own strategies, techniques and approaches. Every serious surfcaster develops his own systems as he evolves into an accomplished fisherman. You must do this as well.

Whatever you may be, a novice or more experienced surf-hand, you can use the techniques mentioned in this book as a starting point or foun-

*The hunt for good bass fishing never ends. Sunrise and the "smoke" of a thousand birds on the water bring hopes of good striper fishing. Learning all the techniques will give you good balance.*

dation upon which you can build. Use it as a blueprint toward new progress, or to add needed weapons to your existing bass-technique arsenal. Every strategy and technique covered here will take you on a journey, an adventure. Every man's situation and condition is his very own, it's unlike anyone else's, and it's for him to figure out what he must do to be effective. What I hope this book does is give you more options and approaches to catch stripers. They will help you tremendously.

If you are good at only one of these techniques, then you are not a well-rounded surfster. This book eliminates any excuses about not being well versed in your approach to the surf. It's a reference book with many starting points that you (add your name here) will refine, experiment with and experience, and only you will decide what is best in the end.

Surfcasters are the smartest and the hardest working of all fishermen. They will make the most out of every possible situation. They will turn a shred of light into a sunbeam, they will take the smallest crack and turn it into a canyon. They will make it happen when no one else can, and they know no one will help them. They have the odds stacked against them; wind, tide, storms, boaters and surfers all rise against the surfster. Yet in the end the surfcaster emerges. A true surfcaster doesn't need a boat to catch a fish. To me, being ready for whatever situation the surf gods throw at you on any particular day is what will make you good, and by good I do not mean the best that there ever was. I mean that you have the capability to do whatever it takes to fool the fish that are in front of you, thus bringing you great satisfaction.

## AN EXCERCISE IN FLEXIBILITY

I was on bass patrol, driving the beach looking for opportunities. It was early June and the big bunker and big bass were starting to show up at various locations along the Jersey Coast. I was looking to get into some good pencil-popping action along the open beaches of northern Ocean County. When the huge schools of adult bunker run along the beach they bring with them bass of the biggest kind. All you need to do is find a bunker school that has bass blowing up on it near the beach, and within casting distance. When this happens your chances for a big fish are often very good.

The problem I encountered on this particular day was a heavy fog moving in and out along the beaches making visibility extremely limited.

It's very hard to see bunker schools when you can't see the water, but the hunt must go on. At about the fifth stop of my patrol, I headed up one of the walkways in Mantoloking and looked south, then north and then south again. I noticed an object in the thick fog. I focused my gaze hard and saw a dark silhouette at the water's edge a short distance away. As it became clearer I saw someone releasing a large striper into the wash that had to be in the high 20s or low 30s. "What's this? Nice!" I thought to myself. Figuring the guy was down about two to three blocks I quickly got to my truck and drove in that direction. I ended up at Lyman Street and quickly made my way up to the wood platform for a look-see. I saw a couple guys at the water's edge, and also a long tidal pool behind them which had formed with the ebbing of the tide. Now the tidal pool is fairly common, but what was uncommon was the pod of hickory shad and bunker that were trapped in the pool with no exit.

I quickly pulled my waders on, grabbed my plug bag and rod, and headed up to the beach. What was happening was clever, yet made com-

*An uncommon situation, a gift from the gods, a tidal pool with bunker and hickory shad made for a good afternoon of livelining.*

mon sense. The guys were snagging shad or bunker from the shallow pool and turning around and walking the bait right into the surf and tossing it in. As soon as the hooked fish made a swim for the deep water, a big blue, or even better, a big bass was waiting for its dinner—an ideal situation. I joined in. It was a perfect big-bass set-up so we kept livelining and catching big bluefish. Everyone there was banking on the take of a big striper. I saw a buddy of mine, friend and longtime striper ace, Shell E. Caris carry off a bass that I believe was about 28 pounds, and he later told me that he released a 30 pounder, plus one that he thought was in the low 40s before I arrived. It was probably Shell that I saw releasing the fish in the fog. The big blues were all over 10 pounds, some pushed close to 20, and unfortunately they were dominating the scene by the time I got into the groove. This scenario was in no way a blitz, but it was true livelining from the sand beach with a God-given livewell to draw fish from.

Another long-time surfcaster bass legend, Mickey Alpert, who just so happened to be on hand this day, beached two of his four 50-pound bass by using this same exact technique of livelining on the open beach. One he caught in 1992 in Spring Lake and another in 1989 on Long Beach Island. He still livelines using this technique today.

This situation is a prime example of how the knowledge and know-how can apply when a particular or unusual situation unfolds before you. A day that I expected to be a plugging day turned out to be a livelining day. Because I knew how to liveline, it was a great advantage and that made the situational transition virtually seamless. Just because a situation develops that is not "textbook" does not mean that it can't be made productive if you as a surfcaster know how to be agile, versatile and ever ready. You must always be prepared for whatever hand you are dealt. My experience with snag-and-drop and livelining both helped in this situation.

## BIG BASS QUEST

If you consider yourself a serious bass man, either there is, or there will come, a time when your fishing interests will turn squarely towards the quest for big bass. Big bass are not commonly caught by most surfcasters, thus the huge appeal. A big fish hoisted onto the scale at the local shop generates a buzz of excitement all around. For the victor it is both a relief,

*A big bass coming out of the night waters is a welcome sight. Finally a pay-off for all the hard work makes a good fish satisfying.*

because the constant pressure of the hunt has finally paid a nice dividend, and it is a time of celebration. You owe this one to yourself for all the hard work you put in. A 10-pound bass will not create the same effect.

The drive to catch big fish in most places along our coast comes in short spurts, perhaps a week, perhaps a couple of weeks, usually never more than a month. It is at this time that activity heightens, and the drive for big bass intensifies to a feverish pitch. Most bass fishers don't get small bass mounted, and I have seen few proud bass men sporting a 4-pound bass in the photo album. It is not the small bass that molest your restful sleep with uneasiness and anxiety. Big bass will have you flopping on your mattress more than a 10 pound bluefish will flop on the beach. Small fish do not consume us, but the mere mention of big fish on the beach spreads along the sea coast towns faster than a brushfire on a windy day. A big bass in your hand says something quite loud.

You may ask, "Are big bass obtainable?" Do you think that you can catch that fish you have always dreamed about? The fish "that other guy caught?" The options available here in this book will give you all the ammo and strategies that you will need to take fish of considerable size.

As always, it will come down to being at the right place at the right time and then doing the right things once you get there. If even one of these three variables is wrong; time, place or technique, it may mean the difference between monster and skunk.

## HOW DO YOU WALK AWAY FROM SUCCESS?

The ability to adapt will make you good. Here is a good example of being flexible. A while back I did quite well chunking from the beach. I consistently hit big fish with many fish in the high 30s, several 40s and even a couple of 50s. The times were good and fishing bunker chunks, at least for me, was the way to the "Promised Land." At this time we had a fair amount of adult bunker in the local waters, but no massive numbers to speak of. The next year we had even more adult menhaden show up and the chunking numbers began to fall. The year after that, we had acres and acres of adult bunker and the big chunk-caught bass dried up. It really made no sense, you would have figured more adult bunker would equal more big bass on the prowl at night looking for an easy meal . . . wrong!

*By knowing what is happening in your area, knowing where the bodies of fish are, and knowing the techniques that are getting the fish keeps you right on the cutting edge. Here Steve Adams grabs a bass.*

As you probably have guessed by now, I am not exclusively a chunker. I like to catch stripers, and I use various techniques and many different approaches to catch them; but one thing should also be obvious by now, and that is the fact that I like to catch big bass. If chunking is what it takes to get it done, then I am a chunker. If they will take artificials, then I plug. Did I keep right on chunking here based on my success of a few years previous? Yes . . . kind of. While I remained faithful to my reliable way of taking big bass, I also got wind of a couple of pals a few miles north of my hunting grounds who were hitting big bass on pencils on a regular basis. These guys were now taking the size fish on artificials that I *was* taking on chunks.

To this day I give these guys a lot of credit as they were open-minded trendsetters. Nobody else was doing this at the time that I know of. I began to listen to what was happening and began to slowly turn my focus away from chunking to another technique, artificials. After another positive report from the northern sector, I made up my mind immediately that a change was in order. Of all the time I was putting into gathering bait and fishing for big bass with no success, I was now eager for a change, especially since big bass were available. I didn't stay married to my recent successes. I was able to adapt. It only took a couple of large bass caught on poppers in and around the bunker schools to make me realize that flexibility was bringing me my success and production. I had crossed the line so to speak. This is the essence of the flexibility that the well-rounded surfcaster needs to be conscious of.

The point here is that regardless of your past success, you can never rest on the throne and fall asleep so to speak. You need to be extremely in tune to the new developments around you at all times.

When you fish, go with what works. Forget about the "rules" that have been laid down before you showed up. You need to constantly keep an open mind as to what you are going to do when you fish tonight. Your biggest downfall will be doing what worked last year, or what your father did, even when those techniques don't work anymore. You will lose your passion when you sit still, you will become complacent once you fall into the rut of a fruitless routine. Listen to what others say, gather their information as a guide, learn their techniques; but be your own fisherman and you will find that the sea and the water offer endless possibilities for catching stripers. There are no limits.

*With a night on the rocks completed, Bill Sistad heads home for breakfast with a nice bass for dinner. By reading water and understanding bass movements wherever you go along the coast you can have success.*

Don't believe that what others preach is right, myself included. Make someone else's theories your realities. I have tried to give foundation blocks for proven striper strategies, but I have not told you that you have to do things this one way or with this one technique. These things don't always work! I have simply given footholds for those who want to grow and develop into great bass men. There is a locked door to the striper world, a world very worthy of discovery. This book holds some of the keys to open the first door, but there will be more doors, and each will open new challenges to you and new levels of excitement and satisfaction.

Your greatest contentment will come as you discover that you are the only one who holds the keys to the locks, and that the road you travel will be your very own. I wish you the best in your endeavors.

# Appendix

Here are a few links to websites with great information about surfcasting and striper fishing. My apologies for any oversights.

Links to great and helpful websites:

www.djmullersurfcaster.com
http://www.superstrikelures.com
http://www.pointjudelures.com
http://www.bigwaterlures.com
http://surfcasting-rhodeisland.com
http://www.afterhoursplugs.com
http://www.lunkercity.com/index.html
http://www.plugcasterlures.com
http://www.surfcaster.com
http://www.weatherunderground.com (great weather info)
http://www.unclejosh.com
http://www.aquaskinz.com
http://www.cottoncordelllures.com
http://www.gibbslures.com
http://www.lamiglas.com
http://www.laptewproductions.com
http://www.vanstaal.com/
http://www.zeebaas.com/
http://www.lurenet.com
http://www.robertslures.com
http://www.gibbslures.com/index
http://www.stripersurf.com/
http://www.stripersonline.com
http://www.striped-bass.com/fishing
http://www.berkley-fishing.com
http://www.stillwater-lures.com
http://www.aoktackle.com

http://www.lighthousesportfishing.com (NJ boat guide Alex Majewski)
http://www.onthewater.com
http://shorelinebt.com/index.html
   (Antique lure site hosted by Tom Clayton)
http://bigrocklures.com/index.html
http://www.realfish-underwater.com/ArtNelsonJerseyShoreVideo.htm
   (Underwater videos on DVD from Art Nelson)

# Index

# About the Author

DJ MULLER was born and raised close to the beach in Manasquan, New Jersey. He now resides there with his wife, Anna, and daughter, Hillary. DJ works in construction and has done so since graduating from Eastern University in 1988.

He spends much of his free time roaming the eastern seaboard in search of striped bass, and writes about his striped bass experiences. His feature stories have appeared in a variety of magazines such as *Saltwater Sportsman*, *The Fisherman*, and *On the Water*. He has a previously published book, *The Surfcaster's Guide to the Striper Coast*.

DJ enjoys traveling, doing seminars and talking about his life as a surf man. DJ also works as a surfcasting guide, and can be contacted at *www.djmullersurfcaster.com*, or email him at *djmull13@msn.com*.